The Ballet Quiz Book

The Ballet Quiz Book

James and
Constance Camner

St. Martin's Press · New York

The rare illustrations are taken from original woodcuts from the *Illustrated London News,* ca. 1840–1860.

Library of Congress Cataloging in Publication Data

Camner, James.
   The ballet quiz book.

   1. Ballet—Miscellanea. I. Camner, Constance.
II. Title.
GV1787.6.C35 1982   792.8   82–6012
ISBN 0-312-06608-2   AACR2

Design by Ed Kaplin

10 9 8 7 6 5 4 3 2 1

First Edition

This book is dedicated to three
friends who gave so much help:

Norman Crider, Tobias Leibovitz, and
Parmenia Migel Ekstrom

MDLLE. CARLOTTA GRISI IN LA ESMERALDA.

ACKNOWLEDGMENTS

We are very grateful to the dancers and balletomanes who helped us with this book and would like to thank in alphabetical order the stars who gave us questions: George Balanchine, Alexander Bennett, Fernando Bujones, Anton Dolin, Parmenia Migel Ekstrom, Carla Fracci, Tamara Geva, Cynthia Harvey, Maria Karnilova, Allegra Kent, Patricia McBride, Ivan Nagy, Walter Terry, and Violette Verdy; and for their help and encouragement, Tobias Leibovitz, Norman Crider of The Ballet Shop, Maitland McDonagh of the Press Department of the New York City Ballet, Anna Sosenko, our editor Ashton Applewhite, Cherryl Lurtsema, our typist, and Carol Mann.

MADAME VESTRIS IN THE NEW DRAMA OF "THE SPEAKING LIKENESS," AT THE PRINCESS' THEATRE.

Contents

Introduction

Okay, so you've seen *Swan Lake* a thousand times and another *Giselle* will make you go mad. You've compared port de bras and counted fouettés, and you always watch for the Blue Bird pas de deux. You are now ready for *The Ballet Quiz Book*.

No college credits or advanced degrees are required, just a love of the dance and an unquenchable curiosity about its stars and its history. The characters and color of a centuries-old tradition are the basis of our book, and the answers—whether you know all or just a few—should surprise, amuse, and edify.

The favorite stars of a ballet-mad world are here as well as many lesser-known lights. There are questions about dancers' greatest achievements and about some rather naughty occasions of the past. We've covered athletes who became dancers, dancers who became choreographers, modern dancers who became ballet stars, and ballet stars who turned to modern dance. We've gone from Paris to St. Petersburg to London to New York City, with stopovers in Copenhagen and Hollywood. The only question was where to begin.

We decided to begin at the end, so to speak, with the greatest stars of today, many of whom contributed their own questions to *The Ballet Quiz Book*. Sprinkled throughout are stumpers from well-known ballet historians and famous dancers about ballet history, their own careers, or just about other dancers, and only true balletomanes will know all the trivia there is to know about the public and private lives of ballet.

To find out just what kind of balletomane you really are, each question or part of a question is assigned a certain number of points. An important note: each question must be answered completely to earn the points, unless points are assigned for parts of the question. You can record your score at the end of each section and match yourself against a ranking system that appears at the end of *The Ballet Quiz Book*.

And now you're ready to jeté into Part I.

The Ballet Quiz Book

MDLLE. DUMILATRE, IN THE NEW BALLET OF "THE CORSAIR," AT DRURY LANE THEATRE.

Part I
Superstar Trivia

We begin with the true superstars of the dance world. You've seen them leap, you've counted their fouettés, you've thrilled to their poetry in motion. Now find out just how much you really know about your favorites.

Chapter One: Baryshnikov

1. A question to stump a carnival barker: How tall is Mikhail Baryshnikov? (6)

2. Baryshnikov's move to the West:
   A. Where did Baryshnikov give his first performance after defecting from Russia? (2)
   B. What was the ballet? (2)

3. How many roles did Baryshnikov dance during his first year in the West? (5)

4. How many roles did Baryshnikov perform in his brief stint with the New York City Ballet? (5)

5. Can you name the town and province in which he was born? (4)

6. What was the first ballet school Baryshnikov enrolled in? (2)

1

7. Mikhail Baryshnikov's gold-medal performance at Varna was a tribute to an equally illustrious dancer. Who was the dancer? (3)

8. A rising star in the ballet firmament sent us this question: "Who did Mikhail Baryshnikov dance his first *Les Sylphides* with in the West?" (6)

9. Baryshnikov delighted American television audiences with his dance spectacular *Baryshnikov on Broadway*, but did you know that he once appeared in a drama on Russian television in a *nondancing* role? Although his performance was in a dramatization of a world-famous novel, we'll give you 25 points if you can name both the role and the novel.

10. Can you name the ballet and the role in which Baryshnikov made his Kirov debut? (5)

11. Most Russian dancers who defect do so for reasons of artistic freedom, but Baryshnikov gave a very different reason on CBS Television's *Sixty Minutes* in 1979. What was it? (6)

12. Few ballets have given Baryshnikov's fans more pleasure than *Push Comes to Shove*. Who choreographed it? (1)

13. Baryshnikov's first attempt at choreography was a hit. What was it? (2)

14. When Baryshnikov "defected" for the second time, from American Ballet Theatre to the New York City Ballet, ABT fans groaned, while City Ballet adherents were overjoyed. Amid all the public discussion of this move, what hardly disinterested party merely noted that, "He is gifted . . . he has good feet"? (2)

15. Did you know that Baryshnikov is a doctor? Where did he receive his degree? (4)

Chapter Two: Makarova

16. Where was Natalia Makarova born? (1)

17. Although Makarova is perhaps most celebrated as Giselle, she has said that she derives more satisfaction from another classical role. Which one? (5)

18. Since leaving the Kirov during its 1970 London tour, Makarova has appeared with many ballet companies. What company has she characterized as having a "Babel-like confusion of styles"? (2)

19. After leaving Russia, Makarova was invited to make her American debut with ABT, and one of her prospective partners was the elegant Erik Bruhn. What was the one prior connection Bruhn had had with Makarova? (4)

20. This question may give you ideas next time you're wondering what to give a prima ballerina for her birthday. What ballet was commissioned as a birthday present for Makarova? (2)

21. For the premiere of Natalia Makarova's historic staging of the Kingdom of Shades, act 4 of *La Bayadère* at the New York State Theater, July 3, 1974, who danced Nikiya (the Bayadère)? (5)

22. Can you name either one of the two dancers who partnered Makarova for her gold-medal-winning performance at Varna? (5)

23. A Russian choreographer Makarova remembers with affection was Leonid Yakobson and no wonder, since it was her creation of a role in a Yakobson ballet that won her the honor of "Best Soviet Ballerina of 1967." Can you name the role and the ballet? (6)

24. While in Russia, Makarova was offered the chance to film *Swan Lake* but turned down the project when the director suggested that she "dance as if you wanted to seduce me." She proudly relates this story and her daring no in her *Dance Autobiography*. Who was the ballerina who eventually starred in the film? (5)

25. It is always exciting when two high-powered temperaments get together in the theater. Could one ask for performers more high-powered than Makarova and opera diva Maria Callas? What opera ballet did Makarova perform under the stage direction of Maria Callas? (5)

26. Who was Makarova's favorite partner while she was at the Kirov? (7)

Chapter Three: The Grand Pas de Deux— Nureyev and Fonteyn

She was the ultimate classical ballerina and the pride of British ballet. He was the enfant terrible of Russian ballet and the most electrifying male dancer since Nijinsky. Separate—superb; together—incomparable!

27. February 21, 1962 will always remain a great moment in ballet history—it was the first time Nureyev danced with Fonteyn. What was the ballet? (2)

28. What was Nureyev's first performance in the United States? (2)

29. When Nureyev made his debut with the Kirov it was

as the partner of a very powerful ballerina, who had specifically requested him. Name her. (5)

30. Margot Fonteyn's name is inseparably linked with that of Sir Frederick Ashton. What was the first of the many wonderful ballets Sir Frederick choreographed for Dame Margot? (7)

31. In what ballet did Nureyev debut as a member of the Kirov? (5)

32. What ballet in the Kirov repertory still retains the modifications Nureyev made while with the company? (2)

33. What occurred while Margot Fonteyn was in Russia with the Royal Ballet that had a profound influence on her career? (2)

34. What did Nureyev answer when Makarova accused him of westernizing his style so that he "danced like them"? (2)

35. Margot Fonteyn made use of many ballet instructors, including the three most celebrated Russian ballerinas teaching in Paris. Can you name the three ballerinas? (6)

36. The legendary Karsavina coached Margot Fonteyn for a role that she warned would be "the most tiring ballet you will ever dance." What was the ballet? (2)

37. Nureyev is now almost as famous for producing ballets as he is for dancing in them. Where did he make his first attempt at producing *(The Nutcracker* pas de deux)? (5)

38. No event has had more of an impact on dance in the West than Rudolf Nureyev's defection from Russia. Here are two questions about that historic event:

    A. What was the first dance company Nureyev joined after his defection? (3)

    B. What was the first American company Nureyev danced with? (3)

39. What teacher could boast of having taught Dame Margot Fonteyn, Anton Dolin, and Dame Alicia Markova? (4)

40. Here is a Nureyev question from ballerina Patricia McBride: "What ballet was created for Nureyev and me?" (4)

41. Did you know that Nureyev's first ballet lessons were given by a former member of the Diaghilev Ballets Russes corps? Take 15 points if you can identify her. (15)

42. Alexander Bennett, former principal dancer of the Royal Ballet, sent us this question about Dame Margot: "Who was the famous violinist who played the adagio in the second act of *Swan Lake* for the pas de deux, when Fonteyn danced Odette with David Blair as Siegfried and me as Benno during the Bath Festival of 1962 in England?" (4)

43. Of all the roles Margot Fonteyn mastered, which did she consider her greatest challenge? (3)

44. Can you name the teacher of Nureyev? (1)

Chapter Four: Pavlova the Swan, and the Legend of Nijinsky

Anna Pavlova took *The Dying Swan* all over the world and became that world's ideal of a prima ballerina; Vaslav Nijinsky's career lasted less than fifteen years, yet his legend is as alive today as it was when he first burst upon the Parisians in 1911.

45. What was the ballet in which Anna Pavlova made her first appearance at the Metropolitan Opera House in 1910? (3)

46. What is the only complete ballet choreographed by Anna Pavlova? (5)

47. What opera company did Pavlova tour with in 1915? (4)

48. In 1916, Pavlova made a full-length film with Universal Pictures, recreating a role originally danced by Taglioni. What was the name of the film? (4)

49. Pavlova's influence on dance was due in part to her frequent tours to every corner of the world. But sometimes her trips to exotic places influenced her own art in unusual ways. She once collaborated with an Indian dancer in choreographing a ballet. You get 4 points if you can name the dancer, and another 8 if you can name the ballet. (12)

50. As Anna Pavlova lay dying, what one thing did she ask for? (3)

51. It is not surprising that Pavlova, the dancer who will be forever identified with swans, had a pet swan of her own. What was the swan's name? (8)

52. Where was Nijinsky born? (4)

53. In 1913, the New York *Tribune* ran the headline: "NIJINSKY SHOCKS PARIS WITH TENNIS DANCE." What was the ballet and who choreographed it? (2)

54. Did you know that Nijinsky's daughter Kyra married an eminent Russian conductor? Name him. (10)

55. What was Nijinsky's wife Romola's maiden name? (3)

56. The last ballet choreographed by Nijinsky was premiered in the United States. Can you name the ballet and the American designer who helped Nijinsky with the conception as well as the designs? (2)

57. Today when a great dancer wants to leave a Russian company, he or she has to defect. But it was easy for Nijinsky—he was fired. Although the incident has never been fully explained, we know that he offended many nobles when he wore a suggestive costume during a 1911 performance at the Maryinsky Theater.
   A. What role was Nijinsky dancing? (2)
   B. Who was his partner? (2)

58. Nijinsky is one of several dancers to be the subject of a ballet. What is the name of this ballet, choreographed by Maurice Béjart, which features extracts from Nijinsky's diary read over a loudspeaker? (3)

Chapter Five: Gala Performance—an Extraordinary Cast of Stars

An extraordinary cast indeed. Keep on your toes, because some of the answers may include the dancers from the four previous chapters.

59. The vastly popular Erik Bruhn always danced to full houses, except on one occasion. What was the performance he gave to an empty house and why? (5)

60. What was Carla Fracci's first role as a ballerina? (7)

61. A grave handicap for any performer is to have a name made famous by another. Imagine the trials faced by an op-

MDLLE. CARLOTTA GRISI AND M. SILVAIN, IN THE NEW BALLET OF "PAQUITA," AT DRURY-LANE THEATRE.

era tenor named Caruso, or a movie star calling herself Garbo. Yet a dancer with a name no less formidable is performing today. Who is the dancer? (2)

62. This question was submitted by a dance celebrity who asks, "What famous ballerina had a father who was a trolley car conductor, and a great uncle who was one of the world's most celebrated opera composers?" (6)

63. Premier danseur Ivan Nagy asks, "Can you name a dozen married couples, past and present, of which both partners were or are internationally known ballet dancers?" (15)

64. Can you name the ballerina who has triumphed despite a deteriorating eye condition throughout much of her career? (1)

65. In what ballet company did Valery Panov first rise to fame? (3)

66. What dancer of recent times has been considered to have the greatest elevation in his leaps? (2)

67. Sometimes the stage is just too small. What ballerina once danced her way right into the prompter's box? (3)

68. What famous dancer made his first stage appearance with the Ufa Opera Ballet? (2)

69. Can you identify the dancer who was born in Bethlehem, Pennsylvania, and who created roles in Balanchine's *Firebird* (the 1970 version), Robbins's *The Goldberg Variations,* and Tudor's *The Leaves are Fading?* (3)

70. Even the greatest dancers have weaknesses. Who was the ballerina whose fouettés in *Swan Lake* were described by a critic as "a Cook's tour of the stage"? (3)

71. What was the first company Cynthia Gregory danced with prior to joining ABT in 1965? (3)

72. The British have a penchant for cloak-and-dagger. What celebrated dancer was introduced incognito, in true James Bond fashion, into a Royal Ballet class as "Mr. Jasmine"? (7)

73. Who was the first American dancer to win a gold medal at the Moscow International Ballet Competition, sometimes known as the "Olympics of Ballet"? (2)

74. Can you identify the dancer who was born in Miami, won a gold medal at Varna, and began his career with the Eglevsky Company in 1970? (2)

75. Shortly after the death of Diaghilev, when it appeared that interest in ballet was fading, three extraordinary young talents came along just in time. Can you identify the three dancers who made phenomenal impressions at such an early age that they were known as the "Baby Ballerinas"? (3)

76. Soviet ballerina Maya Plisetskaya has an equally famous uncle. Can you name him? (3)

77. What was Galina Ulanova's first starring role? (4)

78. What was the first solo role danced by Ulanova? (8)

79. What dancer was the first Soviet citizen to enter France? (5)

80. John Gilpin, British danseur noble, asks: "What was the first role I danced with Ballet Rambert?" (3)

81. It was surely destiny: The parents of a little Russian boy tried to enroll him in the Imperial Naval Academy, but missed the cutoff date, so they took him down the street to the Maryinsky school where at least he would get a similar uniform. In true storybook fashion, the boy became one of the geniuses of the dance. Can you name him? (3)

82. Can you name two ballerinas descended from American Indians? (2)

83. What dancer gave her first contracted performance at the Urania Theater in Budapest? (4)

84. What dancer exclaimed that, "Life would have far more meaning and light if, side by side with the teaching of reading and writing, people were taught to dance beautifully"? (6)

85. No finer American dancer has ever graced the stage than Jacques D'Amboise. Fortunately for future dance lovers, his art has been preserved in several films. Can you name two? (3)

86. Two questions about two of America's geniuses of modern dance:
    A. What city was Isadora Duncan born in? (3)
    B. Where did Martha Graham study dance? (4)

87. What ballerina was called the "Duse of the Dance"? (2)

88. Can you identify the student of June Hampshire who became a member of the Covent Garden Opera Ballet in 1960, and upon joining the Royal Ballet first starred in *Napoli* in 1962? (2)

89. Here are two questions from Fernando Bujones, the

SCENE FROM THE NEW BALLET OF "UNE ÉTOILE," AT THE ROYAL ITALIAN OPERA.

14 · *The Ballet Quiz Book*

brilliant ABT star who won a gold medal at Varna in 1974.
Mr. Bujones asks:
    A. "What ballerina did I perform my first *Le Corsaire*
       pas de deux with?" (2)
    B. "Which solo role did I perform only one time in
       my career as a soloist with ABT?" (8)

90. Can you name the dancer who was born in Brussels;
studied in Copenhagen, Java, The Hague, Caracas, and
Toronto; first danced with the National Ballet of Canada
before joining the Joffrey Ballet; is presently with ABT; and
who won a gold medal at Varna in 1966? (2)

91. Dancers say, "I was born to dance," but maybe the
way they're born makes a difference. Name two wonderful
dancers who were born on a train. (4)

Part I: Answers

Chapter One: Baryshnikov

1. 5′ 7″.

2. A. Canada.
   B. It was a televised performance of *La Sylphide.*

3. 26.

4. 22.

5. Riga, Latvia, in 1948.

6. The Riga Dance School at the age of twelve.

7. The ballet was a tribute to Auguste Vestris, the "dieu de la danse" of the turn of the eighteenth century; *Vestris* choreographed by Yakobson has been repeated by Baryshnikov at galas. (While it is an effective male solo, *Vestris* does not portray eighteenth-century dance technique.)

8. "Cynthia Harvey, Cheryl Yeager, and Kristine Elliott— with ABT." Miss Harvey sent us this question.

9. Baryshnikov was the Toreador in Hemingway's *The Sun Also Rises,* and he reputedly created a sensation in the role.

10. In *Giselle,* not as Albrecht, in which role he has made so great an impression, but in the Peasant pas de deux. One

15

wonders how much he enjoyed his debut, since he has eliminated the Peasant pas de deux from ABT's current production of *Giselle*.

11. "It is impossible to live in a country where people lie to each other every day."

12. Twyla Tharp.

13. His revision of *The Nutcracker* for ABT in 1977.

14. George Balanchine.

15. Yale made Baryshnikov an honorary Doctor of Fine Arts in 1979.

Chapter Two: Makarova

16. Leningrad, Russia.

17. Aurora in *The Sleeping Beauty*.

18. While Makarova is critical of American Ballet Theatre's lack of uniform style, she has also praised the company for its "extreme versatility."

19. Bruhn had been vice-president of the Varna competition in 1965, the year Makarova won a gold medal there.

20. *Other Dances* by Jerome Robbins.

21. Cynthia Gregory.

22. Anatoly Nisnevitch and Vladimir Tikhonov.

23. The Beautiful Maiden in *Country of Wonder*. In her charming *A Dance Autobiography*, Makarova writes that the role "gave me drama and lyricism and the grotesque—everything I have always desired in a role."

24. Elena Evteyeva.

25. Makarova danced under Callas's stage direction in the ballet of *I Vespri Siciliani* at the Teatro Reggio. As if Makarova's appearance in an opera ballet wasn't exciting enough, it was Callas's debut as a stage director.

26. Nikita Dolgushin. Also Makarova's first Albrecht, Dolgushin was a promising soloist until he fell out of favor with the Kirov management and was relegated to the Maly Theater.

Chapter Three: The Grand Pas de Deux— Nureyev and Fonteyn

27. *Giselle.*

28. On television with Maria Tallchief in place of an injured Erik Bruhn, in the pas de deux from *Flower Festival at Genzano*.

29. Natalia Dudinskaya.

30. *Apparitions* in 1936, which she created with Robert Helpmann.

31. *Laurencia,* choreographed by Chaboukiani.

32. *La Bayadère.*

33. Rudolf Nureyev, dancing with the Kirov on their exchange tour in the West, defected in Paris.

34. "No, I dance like me." Nureyev meant that he had formed a style which he considered a combination of the best of East and West.

35. Mathilde Kschessinska, Olga Preobrajenska, and Lubov Egorova. Although many tended to think of these three famed ballerinas as equals in status, Kschessinska, the Assoluta, contemptuously dismissed *their* importance in her memoirs.

36. *The Firebird.* Since Karsavina had created the Firebird in 1910, she was an authority on the subject, but it was nevertheless a triumph for Fonteyn in her 1954 revival.

37. Israel.

38. A. The Ballet International du Marquis de Cuevas.
B. Ruth Page's Chicago Opera Ballet, appearing in Brooklyn in 1962.

39. Princess Serafina Astafieva.

40. "*Le Bourgeois Gentilhomme,* choreographed by Mr. Balanchine for the New York City Opera."

41. Madame Udeltsova.

42. Yehudi Menuhin.

43. Princess Aurora in *The Sleeping Beauty,* the role with which she is most identified.

44. Alexander Pushkin, the incomparable Kirov teacher,

whose students included Semyonov, Soloviev, Panov, and Baryshnikov.

Chapter Four: Pavlova the Swan, and the Legend of Nijinsky

45. *Coppélia.*

46. *Autumn Leaves* (1918).

47. The Boston Opera Company.

48. *The Dumb Girl of Portici* based on the Auber opera, *La Muette de Portici.*

49. Uday Shankar. The ballet was *Radha Krishna.*

50. Delirious, Pavlova asked for her Swan costume.

51. Jack.

52. Although baptized in Warsaw, according to his birth certificate Nijinsky was born in Kiev. There has been some confusion about his place of birth because his dancer parents were on tour at the time. Interestingly, they were also touring in 1891 when Nijinsky's sister, Bronislava, was born. Considering the results, perhaps parents who want their children to become great dancers should stay on the road.

53. *Jeux,* choreographed by Nijinsky.

54. Igor Markevitch.

55. Romola de Pulszky.

56. *Till Eulenspiegel* (1916). The designer was the noted Robert Edmond Jones.

57. Nijinsky was dancing Albrecht to Karsavina's Giselle. Although it is commonplace today, Nijinsky must have indeed shocked the audience when he wore a close-fitting pair of tights giving prominence to certain parts of his anatomy. It was suspected that Diaghilev arranged the incident to free Nijinsky for his own Ballets Russes.

58. *Nijinsky—Clown of God* (1971).

Chapter Five: Gala Performance—An Extraordinary Cast of Stars

59. With unusually bad timing, Bruhn made his stage debut in 1945 on the day German occupation forces surrendered to the British in Copenhagen. It must have seemed that all of Copenhagen, except for the unfortunate young Bruhn, was out on the streets to greet the victorious British soldiers.

60. Cinderella in Alfred Rodrigues's ballet of the same name.

61. Nadezhda Pavlova, star of the Bolshoi, is not related to Anna Pavlova but is a fine ballerina in her own right.

62. Carla Fracci, who sent us the question. The opera composer was none other than Giuseppe Verdi.

63. Mr. Nagy gives us nineteen answers:
Patricia McBride and Jean-Pierre Bonnefous
Marilyn Burr and Ivan Nagy
Felia Doubrovska and Pierre Vladimirov
Toni Lander and Bruce Marks
Vera Fokina and Michel Fokine

Suzanne Farrell and Paul Mejia
Galina Panova and Valery Panov
Marjorie Tallchief and George Skibine
Gisella Caccialanza and Lew Christensen
Nora Kaye and Herbert Ross
Tatiana Riabouchinska and David Lichine
Yekaterina Maximova and Vladimir Vasiliev
Nana Gollner and Paul Petroff
Lubov Tchernicheva and Serge Grigoriev
And for fifteen through nineteen you have Mr. Balanchine and his four wives: Tamara Geva, Vera Zorina, Maria Tallchief, and Tanaquil LeClerq.

64. The remarkable Alicia Alonso has repeatedly triumphed over this seemingly insurmountable obstacle, and is ranked as one of the great ballerinas of this century.

65. The Maly Ballet. It was with this company that Panov impressed Igor Stravinsky as the finest Petrouchka since Nijinsky.

66. Surprisingly, not Baryshnikov, Nureyev, or Bujones, all of whom do have remarkable elevation, but Yuri Soloviev.

67. Natalia Makarova during a performance with the Kirov of *The Bronze Horseman.*

68. Rudolf Nureyev.

69. Gelsey Kirkland.

70. Dame Margot Fonteyn. "A Cook's tour" referred to her less than perfect fouettés, which ideally should be executed on one spot. (Fonteyn, while not always maintaining the required immobility or even attempting all thirty-two fouettés, was nevertheless an exquisite Odile.)

71. The San Francisco Ballet from 1961.

72. Rudolf Nureyev. Fonteyn made up the name.

73. Amanda McKerrow, who was only seventeen at the time of her triumph.

74. Fernando Bujones.

75. Tatiana Riabouchinska, the oldest at fifteen; Tamara Toumanova at fourteen; and Irina Baronova at thirteen. Because Baronova was so young, she was billed as sixteen years old for three years for fear that audiences would not accept so young a dancer. Together, these three remarkable young stars of the Ballet Russe de Monte Carlo helped keep the Western world's interest in dance alive.

76. Asaf Messerer, dancer, ballet master, and choreographer.

77. Maria in Zakharov's *Fountain of Bakhchisaray.*

78. A boy in a wooden shoe dance, in *La Fille Mal Gardée.*

79. Isadora Duncan, a passionate Communist, had taken Soviet citizenship.

80. "The Scotch dance in Ashton's *Façade.*"

81. George Balanchine.

82. Here are three: Rosella Hightower, Maria Tallchief, and Marjorie Tallchief.

83. Isadora Duncan.

84. An idealistic Anna Pavlova. Unfortunately, teaching

THE CAVERNS OF ICE AT THE ALHAMBRA, LEICESTER-SQUARE.

people to dance beautifully is as difficult as teaching people to write beautifully.

85. Here are three: *Carousel, The Best Things in Life Are Free,* and *Seven Brides for Seven Brothers.*

86. A. San Francisco.
      B. At Denishawn, the school run by Ruth St. Denis and Ted Shawn in Los Angeles.

87. Nora Kaye, whose dramatic abilities fully merited the accolade.

88. Anthony Dowell.

89. A. Natalia Makarova.
      B. The Drummer Boy in *Graduation Ball.*

90. Martine van Hamel.

91. Rudolf Nureyev and Tamara Toumanova.

Score:_____

Part II
Choreographers and Companies

Chapter Six: Balanchine, Robbins, and the New York City Ballet

92. What better way to begin a chapter about the New York City Ballet than with a question from the master himself. George Balanchine asks: "What was the first ballet I choreographed in America?" (5)

93. What was the first ballet company Balanchine directed? (3)

94. George Balanchine is rightly celebrated for the classical purity of his ballets, but what extravaganza featuring "fifty elephants and fifty beautiful girls" did he choreograph? (6) Who composed the score? (6)

95. Who first danced the title role in Balanchine's *The Prodigal Son* for:
    A. The Ballets Russes. (4)
    B. The New York City Ballet. (4)

96. Whom has Balanchine called "the most interesting, inventive, and elegant dancer of our time"? (3)

97. The New York City Ballet has been fortunate to possess the talents of two great choreographers: Balanchine and Robbins. What was the first ballet Jerome Robbins created for the New York City Ballet? (4)

98. Who were the original three sailors in *Fancy Free?* (3)

99. What dance company was founded by Jerome Robbins? (4)

100. Here is a question from talented Patricia McBride, star of the New York City Ballet: "In my opinion, what is the greatest gift a dancer can receive?" (4)

101. Can you identify the ballet in which the lovely and seemingly fragile Allegra Kent would carry her male partner off the stage? (2)

102. There are good ballet scores and bad ones, but one so exasperated a critic that he complained that Balanchine could choreograph "from a phone book." What was the ballet? (3)

103. What are the names of the three ballet companies Balanchine has run in the United States? (4)

104. Who composed the score for Balanchine's ballet *Ragtime?* (5)

105. Balanchine's *Jewels* is a ballet in three parts, each representing a different gem. We'll give you 15 points if you can name the three jewels in the order they are presented, and match the jewels to the three composers whose scores are used. (15)

106. A. Who were the first dancers of Balanchine's *Harlequinade Pas de Deux?* (3)
  B. Who were the first dancers of Balanchine's full-length *Harlequinade?* (2)
  C. Who was the Columbine in his third, more expanded version in 1973? (1)

107. Balanchine has been the choreographer for many Broadway shows. Can you name three? (4)

108. Not the least of Balanchine's innovations has been his willingness to collaborate with different companies.
    A. What ballet was jointly presented by the New York City Ballet and the Martha Graham Company? (3)
    B. What company joined the New York City Ballet to present *Concerto for Jazz Band and Orchestra* in 1971? (2)

109. One of Jerome Robbins's undisputed masterpieces is *Dances at a Gathering*. Name all ten of the original dancers who created the work at its premiere. (1 point each, and a bonus of 5 points if you name all ten, for a possible total of 15)

110. Although George Balanchine began his career as a dancer, U.S. audiences have rarely seen him in that capacity. There is one role, however, that he has danced with Suzanne Farrell. What is the role? (2)

111. *Symphony in C* represents some of Balanchine's finest work. Here are a few questions about this important ballet:
    A. What was the original name of the ballet and where was it premiered? (3)
    B. Who composed the score? (2)
    C. Who conducted the first performance? (5)
    D. Who choreographed a different *Symphony in C* for the New York City Ballet? (3)

112. Here is yet another *Symphony in C* question, this from a famous ballerina: "What principal dancer in the New York City Ballet danced the second movement finale steps in *Symphony in C* to the first movement finale music and then ran on again and did the second movement with the right music?" (5)

113. Who composed the score for Balanchine's *Don Quixote?* (6)

114. What did Balanchine reply when Konstantin Sergeyev, then director of the Kirov Ballet, greeted him to Russia with "Welcome to the homeland of the classical ballet"? (3)

115. What New York City Ballet luminary made his debut as an actor with the Yiddish Art Theater in 1937? (3)

116. Jerome Robbins has won two Oscars for what film? (1)

117. A name inseparably connected with Balanchine and the New York City Ballet is that of Lincoln Kirstein, who has been the General Director since 1948. However, Kirstein once directed one company without Balanchine's participation. What was the name of this short-lived but very influential company? (2)

118. One of the most satisfying auditoriums in which to view dance performances is the New York State Theater, since it is one of the few theaters in which the feet of the dancers can be seen from any orchestra seat. Who was the architect who designed it? (2)

119. What was the first home of the New York City Ballet? (3)

Chapter Seven: Americana

From Broadway to ABT

120. American Ballet Theatre gave its very first performance in what theater? (3)

121. What was the first ballet created for American Ballet Theatre that was both a critical and popular success? (5)

122. Who was the first director of American Ballet Theatre? (2)

123. During American Ballet Theatre's tour of Russia, they presented a ballet which an *Izvestia* critic described as a "celebration of livestock breeders in the Southwestern states of the U.S.A." What ballet was that? (3)

124. A star of ballet and Broadway sent us this question: "Who danced the three Dance Hall Girls in the first Ballet Theatre production of Eugene Loring's *Billy the Kid* in 1941?" (5)

125. What famous Hollywood film dancer was asked to choreograph for American Ballet Theatre? (3)

126. Out of what ballet company did American Ballet Theatre grow? (3)

127. The distinguished American writer William Saroyan wrote a ballet-play produced by ABT in 1940. Can you give the name of the ballet and the choreographer? (5)

128. What ballets were created for Ballet Theatre by George Balanchine? (2)

129. Who was the first choreographer to sign a contract to create a ballet for Ballet Theatre? (3)

130. What ABT work was created for an all-black cast? (4)

131. Ballet Theatre has always prided itself on offering a diverse repertory. How many choreographers were featured during their first season in 1940? (3)

132. Here's some real Americana: Can you name the choreographer and the name of the ballet about the doings at a typical gas station? (3)

133. What ballerina was featured in Charles Dillingham's *The Big Show* at the Hippodrome in New York City? (2)

134. Who were the dancers who performed the spectacular "three-legged routine" in the Broadway musical *Blackbirds of 1928?* (6)

135. It is not unusual for a dancer or choreographer to be called brilliant, but one actually earned a Ph.D. in anthropology at the University of Chicago. These studies formed the basis of a career that would include choreographing for Broadway plays like *Emperor Jones,* musicals like *Cabin in the Sky,* and would lead to an important school of dance that, according to the *Concise Oxford Dictionary of Ballet,* was "the cradle of American black dance." Can you name this extraordinary dancer/choreographer/scholar? (3)

136. Tamara Geva, the glamorous ballerina who electrified Broadway in the Rodgers and Hart musical *On Your Toes,* asks: "Who was my co-star in 'Slaughter on Tenth Avenue'?" (3)

137. Who was the featured dancer in the Broadway musical *Shinbone Alley?* (3)

138. What lavish off-Broadway revue featured Martha Graham as a solo dancer? (3)

139. Who was the dancing star of Rudolf Friml's operetta *The Three Musketeers?* (3)

140. Can you name a choreographer who once danced in *West Side Story?* (3)

141. Few Broadway musicals made more of a dancing splash than did Cole Porter's *Can-Can.* Who was the Tony-award-winning choreographer? (2)

142. The ballets by Agnes de Mille for *Oklahoma!* and *Carousel* changed the course of the history of the musical, and for a while it seemed as if every musical presented on Broadway had a de rigueur dream ballet. Who were the featured dancers in *Oklahoma!* and *Carousel?* (2)

143. What ballet was created in place of the proposed *Shore Leave Interlude?* (1)

144. Who is the most famous dancer born in Omaha, Nebraska? (5)

145. One of the great masterpieces of American ballet is Eugene Loring's *Billy the Kid,* to a wonderful score by Aaron Copland. Here are some questions about this work:
   A. What company premiered it? (2)
   B. Who was the first Billy the Kid? (2)
   C. Who was the first Sweetheart? (2)
   D. Who was the first Pat Garrett? (2)

From Hornpipes to Jazz

146. Who was the first famous American male dancer? (3)

147. Can you name the remarkable woman who was the first celebrated ballerina to dance in America, as well as the first woman to choreograph a ballet in America, designing and painting her own scenery? (7)

148. Baryshnikov's performance at the White House was only the most recent of many signs of interest in dance by U.S. presidents. In 1835, Andrew Jackson presented a popular French ballet dancer to Congress, which passed a resolution making her a U.S. citizen. Can you name the dancer? (7)

149. Who was the first American ballerina to make a debut at the Paris Opéra, or, as Théophile Gautier modestly put it, "to seek the approval of Paris, because what Paris thinks is important even to the barbarians of the United States in their world of railroads and steamboats"? (2)

150. Who was the first American-born choreographer to create a ballet for the Paris Opéra? (6)

151. The most important ballet-spectacle of the nineteenth century was *The Black Crook*, first presented in New York in 1866. Not only was it very likely the longest running show of the nineteenth century, but many scholars believe it led to the evolution of the American musical. Here are some *Black Crook* questions:
   A. Who were the four featured ballerinas?
   B. What story was *The Black Crook* based on?
   C. Who choreographed the dances?
   D. How did *The Black Crook* come about?
   E. Where was *The Black Crook* last presented?
   F. What musical starring Jeanmaire was based on the events leading to *The Black Crook?*
   (Don't worry, we realize most of this happened a long time ago, so we'll give you 10 points if you can answer any three of the above questions.)

152. While many people know of Bill Robinson and the Nicholas Brothers, can you name America's first famous black dancer? (6)

153. What is the origin of the dance known as the "Cakewalk"? (3)

154. Did you know that the Metropolitan Opera once annexed a very fine independent ballet company? What was the name of the company and its ballet master? (2)

155. A generation before Isadora Duncan, an American dancer made an international career in modern dance consisting mainly of swirling skirts illuminated by colored lights. Can you name the dancer and her most famous dance? (6)

156. Who was billed as "The Chocolate Nijinsky"? (6)

157. One of the finest American ballet scores is *Appalachian Spring* by Aaron Copland, which premiered in 1944 at the Library of Congress. Who choreographed it? (2)

Chapter Eight: The World of Diaghilev

More than any of the dancers he presented, or the great artists and composers he used, he dominated ballet. It is doubtful that we will ever see another Diaghilev.

158. Diaghilev began his association with art as an editor of a journal in Russia. Name the journal. (6)

159. Who was the featured star ballerina for the first Diaghilev season in Paris and London? (2)

160. Who was the featured star ballerina for the first Diaghilev season in the United States? (7)

161. Who was the highest-ranking ballerina to appear with the Diaghilev Ballets Russes? (3)

162. Diaghilev had a reputation for being cruel at times. He once likened two great ballerinas to opposite sides of the same apple, one of them turned towards the sun, the other in the dark. Who were the ballerinas thus compared? (8)

163. One of the sensations of the first Paris season of the Ballets Russes was *L'Oiseau de Feu* danced by Nijinsky and Karsavina. Who composed the music used for this ballet? (2)

164. Some questions about a famous Diaghilev ballet, *Le Spectre de la Rose:*
    A. Who designed the scenery and costumes? (2)
    B. Who choreographed the ballet? (1)
    C. What is the name of the piano work used for *Le Spectre de la Rose?* (1)
    D. Where was it premiered? (2)

165. Some questions about a ballet forever associated with Nijinsky, *Petrouchka:*
    A. Who wrote the scenario for the ballet? (2)
    B. Who designed the sets and costumes? (2)
    C. Who first danced the role of the Moor? (2)
    D. Where did the premiere take place? (2)

166. In what ballet did Massine make his debut with the Diaghilev Ballets Russes? (4)

167. Before becoming a Broadway star, Tamara Geva was a Diaghilev ballerina. She asks: "What was my first ballet with Diaghilev?" (5)

168. Diaghilev's presentation of the complete *Sleeping Beauty* in London was the first production of this ballet in the West. Who was the unusually distinguished dancer in the role of Carabosse? (4)

169. Who was the star of the first stage presentation produced by Diaghilev outside of Russia? (8)

170. What was the first theater in the United States danced in by the Ballets Russes of Diaghilev? (5)

171. What ballet presented by Diaghilev in the United States aroused the greatest moral objections? (3)

172. Diaghilev reveled in controversy, so what did he do when the audience erupted in fights and shouting matches after the first performance of *L'Après-midi d'un Faune?* (3)

173. Diaghilev saw a Spanish dancer performing in the streets of Seville and was so impressed that he engaged him to help Massine learn the style for the Spanish Dances of *Le Tricorne*. The poor man thought he was going to create the ballet himself and suffered a breakdown when he watched Massine dance the role. He was later found dancing on the altar of a church and was placed in an asylum. Can you name this tragic Spanish dancer? (5)

174. The great Karsavina, not content with her triumphs in dance, appeared as the central character in a play produced in London in 1920. Name the play. (10)

Chapter Nine: Russia before and after Petipa— or, Is There Life after *Swan Lake?*

175. Despite all of the ballets that have been choreographed in Russia, still the favorite of Russian audiences is the old war-horse, *Swan Lake*. Can you answer the following questions?
   A. Who choreographed the first successful version presented at the Bolshoi? (5)
   B. What composer arranged the score for the most popular version, the one choreographed by Marius Petipa and Lev Ivanov? (7)
   C. *Swan Lake* is usually given in four acts. Petipa and Ivanov each choreographed two of the acts. Can you identify which acts were choreographed by which choreographer? (2)

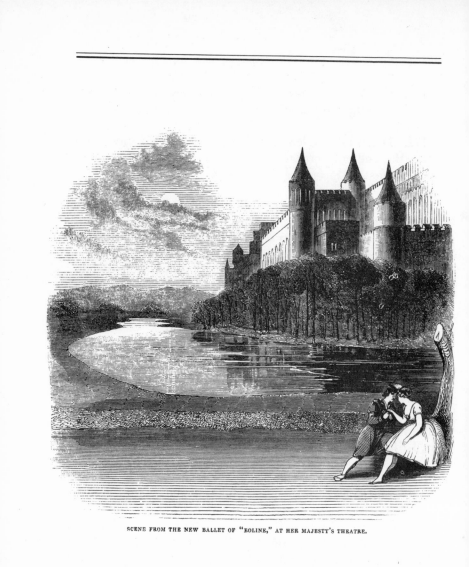

SCENE FROM THE NEW BALLET OF "EOLINE," AT HER MAJESTY'S THEATRE.

D. What ballerina was the first to dance a complete *Swan Lake* in the United States? (5)

176. Who is considered the father of the St. Petersburg (later Leningrad) style? (3)

177. Russian ballet scores form the backbone of today's ballet repertory, but one of the greatest of all Russian composers never composed a score for a ballet. Can you name him? (3)

178. What was the original name of Fokine's *Les Sylphides?* (1)

179. What was the first ballet ever based on Russian folklore? (8)

180. What famous ballet was first presented at the Bolshoi Theater with choreography by Wenzel Reisinger and with Pelageia Karpakova as its star? (5)

181. The grand master of romantic-classical Russian choreography is Marius Petipa. Can you match the dancers in the first column with the Petipa roles they created in the second? (2 points each role, for a total of 14)

1. Carlotta Brianza
2. Maria Petipa II
3. Enrico Cecchetti
4. Pavel Gerdt
5. Pierina Legnani

A. The Blue Bird
B. The Lilac Fairy
C. Princess Aurora
D. Prince Charming
E. Carabosse
F. Odette/Odile
G. Prince Siegfried

182. Some questions about one of the most beloved ballets, *The Sleeping Beauty:*
A. Who is the king who is also the father of Princess Aurora? (5)

    B. Who is the godmother of Princess Aurora? (5)

    C. Can you name all seven of the fairies who dance in the prologue? (9)

183. For the one-hundred-twenty-fifth anniversary of Petipa's birth, a gala performance of *The Sleeping Beauty* was given in Leningrad with a different Aurora for each of the three acts. Name the three Auroras. (9)

184. Every Christmas, ballet companies fill their coffers by performing the Christmas chestnut, *The Nutcracker.* Who wrote the story the ballet is based on? (3)

185. What classic Petipa ballet ends with a spectacular shipwreck? (2)

186. What composer's music is used for Fokine's *The Dying Swan?* (5)

187. Who claimed to be the first dancer to perform the title role in Fokine's *Dying Swan?* (4)

188. Who designed the sets for the famous Royal Ballet production of *The Sleeping Beauty* given in 1946? (2)

189. Who created the title role in Zakharov's *Cinderella* in 1945? (8)

190. The first ballerina to dance Tao-Hoa in *The Red Poppy* has sometimes been called the first great ballerina of the Soviet Union. Who was she? (3)

191. What ballet did Fokine create for Pavlova? (2)

192. Who was the last foreign ballerina to dance at the St. Petersburg Maryinsky Theater? (3)

193. In 1885, a ballerina danced in Russia and made an impression that would influence the course of ballet history. As Alexandre Benois recalled, "Later, collaborating with Diaghilev, creating dramatic ballets instead of the former fairy-tale ballets, I involuntarily recalled the youthful sensations which this marvelous artist produced in me." Can you name the ballerina? (4)

194. What was the first Soviet dance troupe to tour the United States? (2)

195. Name two famous ballet stars who became pillars of the Kirov Ballet, although they had been barred entry to the company's academy. (5)

196. What is the name of the Kirov school, arguably the finest dance academy in Russia? (2)

197. Have you ever gone to a ballet and wondered why people were audibly counting? Of course you have, and the ballet was *Swan Lake* with the inevitable thirty-two fouettés danced consecutively by Odile in act 3. Well, it wasn't always like that:
- A. It was Italian ballerina Pierina Legnani who first astounded St. Petersburg with the virtuoso feat of thirty-two consecutive fouettés. In what ballet? (3)
- B. Naturally, the Russian ballerinas were all jealous of her fabulous feat (no pun intended) and furiously worked to duplicate her achievement. Who was the Russian ballerina who succeeded in being the first to dance the magic thirty-two fouettés? (1)

198. What was the first American ballet company to tour the Soviet Union? (2)

199. During World War II the Kirov was evacuated to Perm, returning to Leningrad in 1944. It left a lasting influence on the Perm State Ballet School. Name two illustrious graduates. (4)

200. Chaboukiani's 1938 ballet *The Heart of the Hills* is to music by a Russian composer named Balanchivadze. Why is that of unusual interest? (3)

Chapter Ten: *Giselle,* and the World of Romantic Ballet

Although it happened over a century and a half ago, our repertory is still dominated by the achievements of the romantic era. What would ballet companies do without *Giselle, La Sylphide,* or *Coppélia?*

201. What contribution to the creation of *Giselle* was not acknowledged in the opening-night program? (6)

202. One of the most underrated ballet scores is *Giselle* composed by Adolphe Adam. Although never ranked with the Tchaikovsky masterpieces or Delibes's scores, its beauty is the perfect setting for the ballet's romantic choreography. Some of the most authentic choreography in the versions we now see, however, is contained in the Peasant pas de deux, which is reputedly unchanged from the original. Ironically, the music for this dance is not by Adam. Can you name the composer? (5)

203. The ballet that really started it all was *La Sylphide.* This was the ballet that made ghostly romances with sylphs and fairies the stock and trade of the romantic ballet. Did you know that the version now most often seen is not the original version that changed ballet history?
    A. Who choreographed the original version? (5)

SCENE FROM THE NEW BALLET OF "ROSIDA," AT HER MAJESTY'S THEATRE.

    B. Who choreographed the version most often seen today? (3)

    C. Who wrote the scenario for the story of *La Sylphide?* (7)

    D. Name the ballerinas who first danced the Sylph in both the original and the most often seen versions. (5)

204. We hope you knew who was the first Sylph, but just in case, we'll tell you that the first Giselle was Carlotta Grisi. But where would those ballerinas have been without the partners that made them appear to float?

    A. Who was the first James in *La Sylphide?* (8)

    B. Who was the first Albrecht in *Giselle?* (5)

205. Now for the story of *Giselle;* since you've probably seen this ballet a dozen times you should know:

    A. The names of Myrtha's two diabolical assistants. (6)

    B. The lady Albrecht is engaged to. (8)

    C. The man who jealously loves Giselle. (1)

206. The lovely Carla Fracci, considered one of the great Giselles of the twentieth century, has had more than twenty celebrated partners in that ballet. Carla Fracci herself asks: "Can you name at least ten of my Albrechts?" (10)

207. *Giselle* has played an important part in Baryshnikov's career. We've already seen that he made his Kirov debut in the ballet. Here are some more questions about this combination:

    A. Who was the Giselle when Baryshnikov danced his first Albrecht? (3)

    B. Baryshnikov's first performance with ABT was in *Giselle.* Who was the Giselle in that historic performance? (1)

C. Baryshnikov's last performance with the Kirov was in *Giselle*. Again, who danced Giselle? (3)

208. This question was sent to us by one of the supreme premier danseurs of the century, Anton Dolin, who wrote: "Who was my first divine Giselle?" (3)

209. Some more *Giselle* firsts:
   A. Who were the first American Giselle and Albrecht? (8)
   B. Who was the first Russian dancer to perform Giselle? (8)
   C. Who first danced Giselle at La Scala? (Hint: She was 13.) (5)
   D. Who was the first Giselle with ABT? (2)

210. Natalia Makarova is one of the great Giselles of our time.
   A. One of Makarova's performances as Giselle was with the greatest of all Soviet danseur nobles as her Albrecht, in the last performance of his career. Who was he? (4)
   B. Who was scheduled to dance Albrecht for Makarova's debut with ABT as Giselle in 1970? (3)
   C. Who actually performed Albrecht for her ABT debut? (2)

211. Our last *Giselle* question: Who were its choreographers? (7)

212. Who choreographed *Coppélia?* (2)

213. Théophile Gautier (1811-1872) is surely the most florid and verbose critic in dance history. What ballet was he referring to when he wrote: "The theme is almost certainly borrowed from the natural history of insects. Virgin ants shed their wings after the love flight . . ."? (2)

214. What role was danced for the first time by a ballerina named Giuseppina Bozzacchi? (7)

215. What was the first romantic ballet to feature the spirit of a dead girl dancing in spooky moonlight? (4)

216. Who was the first ballerina to dance the title role of *La Sylphide* in America? (5)

Marie Taglioni represents the spirit of the romantic ballet. The perfect stylist of her father's choreography, she took her unique beauty of interpretation throughout Europe and Russia, imbuing the world of ballet with a virtually original style. In Paris, however, she shared her stardom with Fanny Elssler.

217. The most bitter ballerina rivalry in ballet history is that which pitted Marie Taglioni against Fanny Elssler. Never at a loss for words, Gautier described one as "Pagan" and the other as "Christian." Which was which? (1)

218. What country can boast that Marie Taglioni was born within its borders? (4)

219. Whom did Marie Taglioni consider her most appreciative audience? (5)

220. The most famous dance performed by Fanny Elssler was her "cachucha," a pseudo-Spanish dance. Take 10 points if you know in which ballet she introduced it. (10)

221. Fanny Elssler had a talented sister who also had a successful career as a dancer. What was her name? (2)

222. In which ballet did Fanny Elssler make her farewell performance? (8)

223. In 1845, ballet history was made by the appearance of four of the greatest ballerinas of the day in Jules Perrot's *Pas de Quatre*. Once a sensation, it languished with the retirement of the dancers it was created for, until Anton Dolin's revival for Ballet Theatre in 1941. Here are some questions:
   A. Who were the four original performers of the *Pas de Quatre?* (5)
   B. The place of honor in such a dance would always be the last variation, the next best place the second to the last, etc. How was the order determined? (2)
   C. Who were the four dancers of Dolin's ABT revival? (8)

224. Dancers are truly beautiful people but one nineteenth-century ballerina was so irresistibly beautiful that she was offered a coffer containing one hundred thousand gold pieces (worth several million today) for her favors. Who was this fabulous beauty? (8)

225. Who was the dancer who was so ugly that his teacher told him to keep moving fast, to keep the audiences from seeing him clearly? (4)

226. Théophile Gautier was not the only writer to use superlatives in describing dancers of the romantic age. W. M. Thackeray described a dancer in his *Roundabout Papers* as "a vision of loveliness such as mortal eyes can't see nowadays." Who was the "vision"? (5)

227. What dancer was known as "La Pointue" for her strong point work? (3)

228. Who were the two nineteenth-century ballerinas who died because their ballet costumes caught fire in the gaslights? (3)

Chapter Eleven: Choreographers and Their Ballets

229. There have been successful women choreographers throughout the history of ballet; as early as the eighteenth century, Marie Sallé was performing in dances of her own creation. Can you name the choreographers of:
  A. *La Vivandiere.* (2)
  B. *Les Biches.* (1)
  C. *Fall River Legend.* (1)
  D. *Le Papillon.* (3)
  E. *Miss Julie.* (1)

230. Who were the two original principal dancers in Antony Tudor's *Pillar of Fire?* (5)

231. What Ashton ballet was created expressly for television *before* World War II? (2)

232. Can you name the Chilean-born ballerina who created the title role in Cullberg's *Lady from the Sea?* (6)

233. Who was the first ballet master to put Stuttgart, Germany, on the ballet map? (3)

234. Who created the title role in Roland Petit's *La Belle au Bois Dormant?* (5)

235. What ballet is based on Victor Hugo's *The Hunchback of Notre Dame?* (2)

236. One of the first choreographers to use classical symphonies (not originally composed for ballet) was Léonide

MDLLE. CERITO, AS LA VIVANDIERE.

Massine. Can you identify the symphonies used for the following "Symphonic Ballets" by Massine?
  A. *Les Présages.* (2)
  B. *Choreartium.* (2)
  C. *Labyrinth.* (2)
  D. *Seventh Symphony.* (2)
  E. *Rouge et Noir.* (2)

237. Who created the choreography for the famous Max Reinhardt production of *A Midsummer Night's Dream* presented at Salzburg in 1927? (6)

238. Maurice Béjart is one of many choreographers to do a version of *Swan Lake,* but with his usual flair, his version is significantly different in two aspects. Can you explain for 6 points? (6)

239. Whose music was used for the Glen Tetley ballet *Tristan,* which starred Rudolf Nureyev? (5)

240. Talk about a dream cast: The premiere for the Kirov's *Creation of the World* boasted a cast any true balletomane would kill to see. We'll give you 10 points if you can identify who portrayed:
  A. God.
  B. The Devil.
  C. Eve.
  D. Adam.

241. Can you name the composer of the ballet that amused lascivious Parisians when the shepherdess, disguised as a male, must bare her breasts to prove she isn't a boy? (5)

242. What ballet was advertised by Sol Hurok as *The Farmer's Daughter?* (3)

243. What ballet has the building of an American railroad as its subject? (3)

244. Who choreographed a ballet about a bedbug? (3)

245. Ballet has always seemed to be a gentle art, but some ballet stories have characters dispatched by gruesome means. If you were a police inspector how would you determine the cause of death in:
  A. *Fall River Legend.* (1)
  B. *La Sylphide.* (2)
  C. *La Bayadère.* (2)

246. Did you know that there is a ballet based on a horror story by Edgar Allan Poe? Name the story and the ballet. (3)

247. What was the ballet Sir Frederick Ashton choreographed for the Royal Ballet's celebration of the four-hundredth anniversary of Shakespeare's birth? (3)

248. What is the oldest ballet to survive with original choreography? (3)

249. All dancers have endured the rigors of dance class. What ballet is based on a nineteenth-century ballet class? (2)

250. What famous ballet was last performed in its original version in 1868? (3)

251. Perhaps the most popular source for ballet stories is Shakespeare's *Romeo and Juliet.* We found the names of twenty-four choreographers who have fashioned ballets on the *Romeo and Juliet* story. Can you name ten? (12)

252. Who was the first to choreograph a ballet to Prokofiev's *Romeo and Juliet* score? (5)

253. The ballet *Apollon Musagète* was premiered on April 27, 1928.

> A. Who was the choreographer? (2)
> B. What theater was used? (6)

254. Mikhail Baryshnikov has expressed admiration for many choreographers but there is one of whom he said, "If we could get him, I'd give him Ballet Theatre!" Who is this obviously special choreographer? (2)

255. What is the name of the ballet spectacle that dramatized the struggle between progress, represented by inventions like electricity, and the forces of ignorance? (3)

256. What is the name of the Massine ballet that was based on sketches in *The New Yorker* magazine? (4)

257. Eliot Feld's first ballet was *Harbinger* produced in 1967 by what company? (4)

258. Johann Sebastian Bach never wrote a ballet, but you'd never know it from all the Bach scores that have been choreographed in the twentieth century. Name five ballets to music by Bach. (4)

MADAME CELESTE'S FAREWELL APPEARANCE IN THE "QUEEN'S SECRET."—(SEE PRECEDING PAGE.)

Part II: Answers

Chapter Six: Balanchine, Robbins, and the New York City Ballet

92. Mr. B's answer: *"Serenade* (music by P. I. Tchaikovsky, Serenade for Strings in C, op. 48)."

93. Les Ballets, in Paris in 1933.

94. *The Circus Polka* for the Barnum and Bailey Circus was first produced at Madison Square Garden in 1942 to music by Stravinsky. It was performed over four hundred times.

95. A. Serge Lifar.
B. Jerome Robbins.

96. Fred Astaire.

97. *The Guests.* Produced in 1949, this was an abstract treatment of *Romeo and Juliet.*

98. Jerome Robbins, John Kriza, and Harold Lang.

99. Ballets: U.S.A. (1958).

100. "To have a ballet created for you by a great choreographer." As Miss McBride explained, "I've been lucky! Ballets are gifts and I've been the instrument for Balanchine and Robbins in many ballets. I've loved them all: *Harlequinade*

with Eddie Villella, Rubies in *Jewels, Tarantella, Who Cares?,
Dances at a Gathering,* and so many more."

101. *Night Shadow* (also known as *La Sonnambula)* choreographed by Balanchine.

102. *Agon,* to an atonal Stravinsky score that Balanchine
has called "appetizing."

103. The American Ballet, the Ballet Society, and the
New York City Ballet.

104. Igor Stravinsky.

105. Part 1. Emeralds, to music by Gabriel Fauré.
Part 2. Rubies, to music by Igor Stravinsky.
Part 3. Diamonds, to music by Tchaikovsky.

106. A. Maria Tallchief and André Eglevsky.
B. Edward Villella and Patricia McBride.
C. Gelsey Kirkland.

107. Here are four: *The Ziegfeld Follies, On Your Toes, I Married an Angel,* and *Song of Norway.*

108. A. *Episodes.* Martha Graham and Balanchine each
choreographed ballets of the same name that
were presented back-to-back. Paul Taylor starred
in the Balanchine portion and Graham used New
York City Ballet dancers in hers.
B. The Dance Theater of Harlem. New York City
Ballet alumnus Arthur Mitchell choreographed
the ballet with Balanchine.

109. Allegra Kent, Sara Leland, Kay Mazzo, Patricia
McBride, Violette Verdy, Anthony Blum, Robert Maiorano,
John Prinz, Edward Villella, and John Clifford.

110. Sancho Panza in his ballet *Don Quixote.*

111. A. *Le Palais de Cristal,* premiered at the Paris Opéra in 1947.
B. Georges Bizet.
C. Balanchine.
D. John Clifford. His ballet is set to a Stravinsky symphony.

112. Allegra Kent wrote us, "Yep! It was yours truly. The conductor wasn't told of the cut or something, so I had the weirdest look on my face, a mixture of laughing, crying, surprise, and shock!"

113. Nicolas Nabokov.

114. "No," replied Balanchine, "the homeland of the classical ballet is New York."

115. Jerome Robbins.

116. *West Side Story* for direction and choreography, in 1962.

117. Ballet Caravan. Founded by Kirstein in 1936 as a showcase for young American choreographers, this company made history before it was disbanded in 1941.

118. Philip Johnson.

119. The New York City Center for the Performing Arts, 1948 to 1963.

Chapter Seven: Americana

120. Rockefeller Center Theater in Radio City, New York, on January 11, 1940.

121. *Bluebeard* by Michel Fokine. With a cast including Dolin, Markova, and Baronova, this ballet delighted the opening night audience at the Palacio de Bellas Artes in Mexico City, in 1941.

122. Richard Pleasant.

123. *Rodeo* by Agnes de Mille.

124. "Miriam Golden, Mimi Gomper, and Maria Karnilova." Miss Karnilova, star of the current run and the original production of *Fiddler on the Roof,* kindly sent us this question.

125. Gene Kelly; unfortunately, he has yet to do so.

126. The Mordkin Ballet founded by Mikhail Mordkin in 1926.

127. *The Great American Goof* was choreographed by Eugene Loring.

128. *Waltz Academy* and *Theme and Variations.*

129. Michel Fokine.

130. *Black Ritual* by Agnes de Mille was danced by their "black wing" in ABT's very first season. The black wing was dropped when *Black Ritual* went out of the repertory the next season.

131. Eleven.

132. *Filling Station* was choreographed by Lew Christensen in 1938 to a score by Virgil Thomson. This story about Mac, the gas station attendant, was an important precursor to American theme ballets like *Billy the Kid, Rodeo,* and *Fancy Free.*

133. Anna Pavlova.

134. Bill "Bojangles" Robinson and Peg Leg Bates. The amazing Bates, with his one artificial leg, fully kept up with the fabled Robinson. Peg Leg Bates claims that it was on that occasion that Robinson received his first standing ovation. Bates, a fashion plate, reportedly had a different peg leg to match each of his many suits.

135. Katherine Dunham.

136. "Ray Bolger." "Slaughter on Tenth Avenue" is the ballet from *On Your Toes* that made Broadway history. It was choreographed by George Balanchine.

137. Allegra Kent.

138. *The Greenwich Village Follies.*

139. Harriet Hoctor, who made a sensation in her solo, "Ma Belle."

140. Michael Bennett, talented choreographer of *A Chorus Line.*

141. Michael Kidd.

142. Joan McCracken as "the girl who fell down" in *Oklahoma!* and Bambi Linn as Louise in *Carousel.* Linn also appeared in *Oklahoma!*'s first production as Aggie.

143. *Fancy Free.*

144. Fred Astaire.

145. A. Ballet Caravan.
B. Eugene Loring.

    C. Marie-Jeanne.
    D. Lew Christensen.

146. John Durang (1768-1822). Famous for his hornpipe dances, he later excelled in classical ballet.

147. Suzanne Théodore Vallande Douvillier (1778-1826) was billed as "Madame Placide" on her American tours, making her debut in New York at the John Street Theater in 1792. She staged her own *Echo and Narcissus* in 1796.

148. Mlle Celeste (1811-1882).

149. Augusta Maywood (1825-1876). Gautier grudgingly admitted she was a "good acquisition."

150. Gene Kelly. It was *Pas de Dieux* to music by Gershwin in 1960.

151. A. Maria Bonfanti, Rita Sangalli, Betty Rigl, and Rose Delval.
    B. The opera *Der Freischütz* by Weber.
    C. David Costa.
    D. A theater troupe and a French ballet company were forced to use the same theater because of a double-booking, so they devised an entertainment both could participate in.
    E. Hoboken, N.J., in 1929. Agnes de Mille produced it.
    F. *The Girl in Pink Tights* (1954), to a Romberg score.

152. Juba (William Henry Lane), born in 1825. His dancing was described as featuring "flexibility of joints." He was a smash hit in Europe.

153. The Cakewalk was a famous dance of minstrel shows

of the nineteenth century. The name derives from the cake awarded to the dancer who executed the most dazzling steps.

154. The American Ballet with Balanchine as ballet master. The company even performed the opera *Orfeo ed Euridice,* the dancers providing all of the movement and the singers singing in the wings. This noteworthy experiment was condemned by critics, and Lincoln Kirstein later summed up the venture with the observation that "Ballet and Opera rarely mix . . . ," apparently discounting the history of opera and ballet in France.

155. Loie Fuller, most famous for her *Serpentine Dance.* This world-famous dance star of the 1890s made some primitive films which show that she was quite an effective performer, and her contribution to modern dance appears to be underrated.

156. Bill "Bojangles" Robinson, most legendary of tap dancers.

157. Martha Graham.

Chapter Eight: The World of Diaghilev

158. *Mir Iskusstva* (The World of Art).

159. Anna Pavlova.

160. One Xenia Maclezowa, who was said to be "from Moscow." American audiences were avid to see the Diaghilev stars they had read about, Nijinsky and Karsavina. But Nijinsky was interned in Budapest, not making his American debut until four months later, and Karsavina was pregnant and unavailable for the U.S. tour. It was the delightful

Lydia Lopokova who emerged as the favorite of American audiences.

161. While many great ballerinas appeared with Diaghilev, only one Prima Ballerina Assoluta (as officially designated by the czar) danced with Diaghilev's company—Mathilde Kschessinska.

162. Olga Spessivtseva and Anna Pavlova. Pavlova got the short or dark end of the comparison, and never forgave Diaghilev for it.

163. Tchaikovsky. It was a pas de deux and its success inspired the full-length ballet composed by Stravinsky.

164. A. Léon Bakst.
B. Michel Fokine.
C. *Invitation to the Dance* by Weber, but orchestrated by Berlioz.
D. Monte Carlo in 1911.

165. A. Alexandre Benois.
B. Alexandre Benois.
C. Alexandre Orlov.
D. Paris in 1911.

166. *La Légende de Joseph* choreographed by Fokine.

167. *"Le Train Bleu* with Anton Dolin."

168. Carlotta Brianza, the original Maryinsky Aurora in 1890, danced the first Diaghilev-produced performances as Carabosse, before the role was taken over by Enrico Cecchetti, the Carabosse in the 1890 Maryinsky production.

169. Legendary Russian bass Feodor Chaliapin in *Boris*

Godunov. This production so impressed the management of the Metropolitan Opera that they bought all of the sets and costumes and used them when they first presented the opera.

170. The Century Theater, in New York City.

171. *Sheherazade,* because of the implication of miscegenation.

172. He ordered the curtain raised and encored the entire ballet.

173. Felix Fernandez Garcia.

174. *The Truth About the Russian Dancers.*

Chapter Nine: Russia before and after Petipa— or, Is There Life after *Swan Lake?*

175. A. Alexander Gorsky in 1901.
  B. Riccardo Drigo, because Tchaikovsky had died the previous year.
  C. Petipa, acts 1 and 3; Ivanov, acts 2 and 4.
  D. Yekaterina Geltzer.

176. Charles-Louis Didelot (1767-1837) was ballet master in St. Petersburg from 1801 to 1811 and from 1816 to 1837.

177. Modest Mussorgsky.

178. *Chopiniana.*

179. *The Humpbacked Horse,* choreographed not by a Russian, but by Arthur Saint-Léon while ballet master in St. Petersburg.

180. *Swan Lake.* Tchaikovsky was bitterly disappointed by the failure of this production and it remained for Petipa and Ivanov to bring his score to life.

181. 1. C   2. B   3. A, E   4. D, G   5. F

182. A. King Florestan XXIV.
B. Carabosse, who does not behave like a loving godmother when they forget to invite her to the christening.
C. The Lilac Fairy.
The Fairy of the Crystal Fountain.
The Fairy of the Enchanted Garden.
The Fairy of the Woodland Glades.
The Fairy of the Songbirds.
The Fairy of the Golden Vine.
Carabosse.

183. Act 1. Marina Semyonova.
Act 2. Galina Ulanova.
Act 3. Natalia Dudinskaya.
As if the presence of the three ballerinas wasn't enough, the fabled Yekaterina Geltzer played one of the queens. This dreamlike gala occurred on May 22, 1947.

184. E. T. A. Hoffmann. The story was *Der Nussknacker und der Mäusekönig.* Another classic, *Coppélia,* is based on his story *Der Sandmann.*

185. *Le Corsaire.* Originally choreographed by Mazilier in 1856, it was rechoreographed by Petipa. Western audiences are most familiar with the marvelous pas de deux from Petipa's full-length version.

186. Camille Saint-Saëns's *Le Carnaval des Animaux.*

187. Lydia Kyasht, a Maryinsky Theater soloist, claimed

SCENE FROM THE NEW BALLET OF "LE CORSAIRE," AT HER MAJESTY'S THEATRE.

to have been the first to dance the ballet that was created for Pavlova for a St. Petersburg gala.

188. Oliver Messel. The sets were so well remembered that ABT recently recreated them for their own production of *The Sleeping Beauty.*

189. Olga Lepeshinskaya.

190. Yekaterina Geltzer (1876-1962). The remarkable Geltzer had strong dramatic gifts and was considered the perfect Gorsky ballerina.

191. *The Dying Swan.*

192. Carlotta Zambelli (1875-1968). She danced at the Maryinsky in 1901. A star at the Paris Opéra for many years, she became an imposing teacher and was addressed as "Grande Mademoiselle."

193. Virginia Zucchi (1847-1930).

194. The Moiseyev Folk Dance Ensemble in 1958.

195. Konstantin Sergeyev and Vakhtang Chaboukiani, as well as Sergei Koren and Leonid Yakobson, received ballet training at the evening courses of the Leningrad Ballet School because they were past the required entrance age for the regular classes. Sergeyev went on to become the supreme Russian danseur noble and, eventually, the director of the Kirov. Chaboukiani typified the virile Soviet dancer of heroic twentieth-century ballets.

196. The Vaganova School named for the revered teacher Agrippina Vaganova (1879-1951) whose method crystalized the best qualities of the Soviet style.

197. A. *Cinderella.* But by incorporating them into her performances of *Swan Lake,* Legnani set a tradition that remains.
   B. Mathilde Kschessinska, in *Swan Lake.*

198. American Ballet Theatre in 1960.

199. Nadezhda Pavlova and Galina Panova.

200. The composer was the brother of George Balanchine.

Chapter Ten: *Giselle,* and the World of Romantic Ballet

201. The principal choreographer, Jules Perrot, did not even have his name listed in the program.

202. Friedrich Burgmüller.

203. A. Filippo Taglioni, for his daughter Marie.
   B. August Bournonville.
   C. Adolphe Nourrit, remembered as a great opera tenor.
   D. Marie Taglioni was the first. Lucile Grahn first danced the Bournonville version that we usually see today.

204. A. The first James was Joseph Mazilier.
   B. Lucien Petipa, brother of the better-known Marius, was the first Albrecht.

205. A. Moyna and Zulma.
   B. Bathilde, daughter of the Duke of Courland.
   C. Hilarion.

206. Miss Fracci gives us more than enough names to an-

THE FAREWELL.—CARLOTTA GRISI AND PETIPA, IN
THE "PERI."

swer the question: "Erik Bruhn, Rudolf Nureyev, Paolo Bor-
toluzzi, Ted Kivitt, Vladimir Vasiliev, Ivan Nagy, Mikhail
Baryshnikov, Royes Fernandez, Fleming Flindt, John Gilpin,
Mario Pistoni, Alexander Godunov, Lawrence Rhodes, James
Urbain, George Janco, Giulio Perugini, Gianni Notari, etc."

207. A. Alla Sizova.
   B. Natalia Makarova.
   C. Natalia Bessmertnova.

208. "It was Olga Spessiva (Spessivtseva) in London, June
1932." The precious film of Spessivtseva and Dolin dancing
Giselle shows that she was indeed a divine Giselle.

209. A. It was first performed in America with an all-
   American cast: Mary Ann Lee (1823-1899) and
   George Washington Smith (1820-1899) were the
   Giselle and Albrecht. Interestingly, Smith began
   his career as a clog dancer until Fanny Elssler
   spotted him and included him in her American
   tour.
   B. Yelena Andreyanova, in 1842.
   C. Sofia Fuoco (1830-1916).
   D. Annabelle Lyon.

210. A. Konstantin Sergeyev.
   B. Erik Bruhn, who had to bow out due to an injury.
   C. Ivan Nagy.

211. Jules Perrot and Jean Coralli choreographed *Giselle*.
Perrot choreographed all of Giselle's dances for his wife Carlotta Grisi. Coralli choreographed the rest of the ballet.

212. Arthur Saint-Léon.

213. *La Sylphide.*

214. Swanilda in *Coppélia*. Bozzacchi was another of those brilliant young dancers of the romantic era whose careers were tragically cut off. She died at the age of seventeen, during the devastating siege of Paris by the German army in 1870.

215. The act 3 ballet in Meyerbeer's opera, *Robert le Diable*. This "Dance of the Ghostly Nuns" was created by Marie Taglioni.

216. Mlle Celeste in 1835.

217. The "Pagan" was Elssler, the "Christian," Taglioni, a reference to the former's sensuality and the latter's purity. Gautier was very impressed with the physical beauty of Elssler and wrote a long, lecherous description of her legs. Despite the many years that have elapsed since the careers of Marie Taglioni (1804-1884) and Fanny Elssler (1810-1884), the argument still rages between the "Elsslerists" and "Taglionists" about who was the better dancer. What do you think?

218. Sweden.

219. A band of robbers who once waylaid her in Russia and made her dance for them. Although she was carrying a valuable jewelry collection, the brigands only confiscated as a souvenir the rugs she had put down to dance upon.

220. *Le Diable Boiteux* by Coralli.

221. Therese. Her only drawback was that she was too tall, a complaint which still causes grief to dancers.

222. *Faust,* choreographed by Perrot.

223. A. Marie Taglioni, Fanny Cerrito, Carlotta Grisi, and Lucile Grahn.
   B. By age. When this formula was agreed upon, the dancers were suddenly very reluctant to claim their rightful places.
   C. Nana Gollner, Nina Stroganova, Alicia Alonso, and Katherine Sergava.

224. Pauline Duvernay (1813-1894), who turned the offer down. She did tell another suitor that she would accept his middle tooth for her favors. When the gentleman returned with a bloody mouth and the tooth in his hand, she laughed at him: "I asked for a lower tooth and you brought me the upper." There is no record of whether the poor man tried again.

225. Jules Perrot (1810-1892) became the leading dancer of the day despite his looks. The advice was given to him by Auguste Vestris.

226. Pauline Duvernay, again.

227. Sofia Fuoco (1830-1916).

228. Clara Webster (1821-1844) and Emma Livry (1842-1863). The cruel deaths of these ballerinas along with that of Bozzacchi are among the reasons now cited to explain the eclipse of the romantic ballet.

Chapter Eleven: Choreographers and Their Ballets

229. A. Fanny Cerrito.
   B. Bronislava Nijinska.
   C. Agnes de Mille.
   D. Marie Taglioni.
   E. Birgit Cullberg.

THE NEW DANSEUSE, EMMA LIVRY.

230. Nora Kaye and Hugh Laing.

231. *First Arabesque* starring Margot Fonteyn in 1937.

232. Lupe Serrano.

233. Jean-Georges Noverre was ballet master in Stuttgart from 1759 to 1766. Like the princess in *Sleeping Beauty,* Stuttgart's ballet went to sleep until awakened by John Cranko in 1961 in what has been called "The Stuttgart Ballet Miracle."

234. Leslie Caron.

235. *La Esmeralda,* choreographed by Jules Perrot, was a standard work in nineteenth-century repertoires. The last famous Esmeralda was Mathilde Kschessinska who considered it her favorite role. Kschessinska, who died in 1971, often wondered why the ballet was not revived. So do we.

236. A. Tchaikovsky's Fifth Symphony.
    B. Brahms's Fourth Symphony.
    C. Schubert's Seventh Symphony.
    D. Beethoven's Seventh Symphony.
    E. Shostakovich's First Symphony.

237. Tilly Losch, Viennese actress and dancer who also performed in the play.

238. Unlike all of the other versions, Béjart did not use Tchaikovsky's music, but the score of Beethoven's Ninth Symphony; perhaps even more original is his Swan Queen, portrayed by a man!

239. Not Wagner's, but that of Hans Werner Henze.

240. A. God was portrayed by Yuri Soloviev.
    B. The Devil was Valery Panov.

C. Eve was Irina Kolpakova.
D. Adam was Mikhail Baryshnikov.
The ballet was choreographed by Kasatkina and Vasiliov in 1971.

241. Wolfgang Amadeus Mozart. The ballet was *Les Petits Riens*, choreographed by Noverre. Mozart was very resentful when Noverre added the music of other composers to the ballet.

242. Ashton's *La Fille Mal Gardée.*

243. *Union Pacific*, choreographed by Massine in 1934.

244. Soviet choreographer Leonid Yakobson choreographed *The Bedbug* in 1962 for the Kirov Ballet.

245. A. It was an axe murder. *Fall River Legend* tells the story of Lizzie Borden.
B. By means of an enchanted scarf which causes the Sylphide's wings to fall off. (If you said death was due to loss of wings, take the points.)
C. The bayadère Nikiya is killed by a snake bite.

246. *Usher*, choreographed by Léonide Massine and first produced in Buenos Aires in 1955, is based on Poe's classic *The Fall of the House of Usher.*

247. *The Dream*, based on *A Midsummer Night's Dream.* This ballet made Antoinette Sibley and Anthony Dowell stars when it premiered in 1964.

248. *The Whims of Cupid and the Ballet Master* choreographed by Galeotti was first performed in Copenhagen, Denmark, in 1786. The Royal Danish Ballet has frequently revived it.

249. *Konservatoriet.* This popular Bournonville ballet, first performed in 1849, is still in the repertory. The ballet takes place in a class in the Paris Conservatory run by Vestris.

250. *Giselle.* The ballet we now see is an adaptation by Marius Petipa for the St. Petersburg Maryinsky Theater. No one can be sure just how much Petipa changed the choreography, although the first Albrecht was his brother. However, there is little doubt that Petipa's version is considerably different from what was originally presented. Descriptions of the original choreography for *Giselle* just do not tally with what we now see.

251. Leonid Lavrovsky, Oleg Vinogradov, Ivo Psota, Nicolai Boyartchikov, Margarita Froman, Sir Frederick Ashton, John Cranko, Kenneth MacMillan, Rudi van Dantzig, John Neumeier, Eusebio Luzzi (Venice 1785), Vincenzo Galeotti, Bronislava Nijinska, George Balanchine, Birger Bartholin, Gyula Harangozó, Victor Gsovsky, Serge Lifar, Antony Tudor, George Skibine, Erich Walter, Maurice Béjart, Gray Veredon, and Rudolf Nureyev are just a few of the countless choreographers. Take the points if you came up with ten of the above or others. In fact, we'll allow Jerome Robbins for *West Side Story.*

252. Ivo Psota at Brno, Czechoslovakia, December 30, 1938.

253. A. The choreographer was Adolph Bolm.
    B. The performance was given at the Library of Congress in Washington. Balanchine's well-known ballet, sometimes just called *Apollo,* choreographed to the same Stravinsky score was presented two months later in Paris.

254. Jiři Kylián, who has assumed the most-promising-

THE MINUET DE LA COUR.

choreographer position after John Cranko's tragically early death.

255. *Excelsior,* produced at La Scala in 1881. Typical of the spectacular genre epitomized by *The Black Crook* and its lavish sets, frequent magical scene changes, and lots of dancers, *Excelsior* enjoyed a popularity in Europe that lasted more than thirty years. Hopelessly dated, the ballet's recent revivals have been less successful.

256. *The New Yorker* which premiered in New York in 1940, with a remarkable cast including Danilova, Eglevsky, Massine, and Franklin.

257. ABT.

258. Here are more than enough to answer the question:
Nijinska's *Étude*
Fokine's *Les Éléments*
Balanchine's *Concerto Barocco*
Lifar's *Dramma per Musica*
Petit's *Le Jeune Homme et la Mort*
Charrat's *Diagramme*
Gore's *Night and Silence*
Macdonald's *Aimez-vous Bach?*
Harkarvy's *Recital for Cello and Eight Dancers*
Cranko's *Brandenburg nos. 2 & 4*
Béjart's *Actus Tragicus*
Robbins's *The Goldberg Variations*
Taylor's *Esplanade*

Score: _____

Part III
Bouquets

Chapter Twelve: Historical Anecdotes and a Smattering of Technique

In this chapter we will explore how much you know about the people who started it all. Although not as well known as the characters of the Diaghilev period or the romantic ballet, the pioneers of the early days of ballet are even more colorful. Scattered among the historical anecdotes are questions concerning ballet steps. Assuming you know there are five positions in ballet, we will quiz you on your technique; you only have to name certain steps, however, not execute them. If you pay attention you'll learn how one dancer discovered the secret of preserving her youthful looks for over thirty years.

259. Let's start at the beginning. The first performance of ballet as we know it took place in 1581 by commission of Catherine de Medici. Take 10 points if you can name the ballet and/or the choreographer. (10)

260. What was the first dancing academy and who established it? (4)

261. This question was sent to us by Parmenia Migel Ekstrom, noted ballet historian and author of the informative and delightful *The Ballerinas:* "Marie Taglioni is often given the credit for being the first ballerina to dance on *pointe.* Name three dancers who preceded her as exponents of this technique." (8)

262. Here's another tough question from Mrs. Ekstrom: "Famous dancers often have sons who follow their fathers' profession. Name one father-and-son of the eighteenth, nineteenth, and early twentieth century, and today." (four fathers-and-sons in all, for 10 points)

263. Opera divas Giuditta Pasta and Maria Malibran advised a young dancer to forsake her ballet career for the opera stage. Who was the ballerina? (3)

264. What was the first ballet to feature a professional ballerina (as women's roles had hitherto been taken by ladies of the nobility or by young men)? (8)

265. A dancer's greatest enemy is not pulled tendons or sprained muscles, but advancing age. Many a dancer has had cause to regret the loss of physical agility and youthful appearance at the time artistic maturity is reached. However, one dancer seemed to have found a fountain of youth, since twenty years into her career, it was said she looked as she had for her debut. What was Marie-Madeleine Guimard's secret? (8)

266. Who is credited with being the first ballerina to use the blocked toe slipper? (3)

267. Who invented the pirouette? (8)

268. Talk about bragging, here is what a dancer said about his son: "My son only comes down out of the air to the stage out of consideration for his fellow dancers!" Can you name the father and the son? (4)

269. What was the problem that prevented Mlle Clotilde from obtaining a dancing partner, even though she possessed a technique described by the strict Noverre as perfect? (6)

270. What was the first celebrated rivalry between two ballerinas? (4)

271. Can you name the first true ballet to be performed in the United States? (Hint: It was produced in New York in 1792.) (10)

272. What was the legal way to abduct a girl in Paris during the eighteenth century? (5)

273. Who was the first male dancer to perform without a mask in ballet? (3)

274. What ballet step is often compared to the stitches made by a sewing machine? (2)

275. What ballet step takes its name from a cat's movement? (1)

276. All female dancers who wear panties conform unknowingly to a police ordinance enacted in Paris in the eighteenth century. Why was this ordinance needed? (3)

277. Dance has had many peculiar manifestations, but one tradition includes dancing horses. What was a seventeenth-century ballet called that featured the performance of horses? (3)

278. What great composer appeared as a dancer in some of the ballets he composed? (7)

279. What celebrated nineteenth-century dancer composed music for some of his ballets? (3)

280. What does it mean in French ballet terms to be called a "rat"? (5)

281. Everyone knows that Nijinsky was called the "God of the Dance." Can you name three earlier male dancers who were also called gods of the dance? (6)

282. The saying that "you can never be too rich or too thin" has always applied to dancers. One in particular was so thin that a noted wit observing her performance as a nymph between two fauns said the scene reminded her of "two dogs fighting for a bone." Who was this celebrated dancer? (Hint: One of the fauns was the great Vestris.) (4)

283. Although best known for *The Legend of Sleepy Hollow* and *Rip Van Winkle,* American writer Washington Irving was a balletomane. He described what ballet step as "pigeon's wings"? (3)

284. Who was the dancer whose name is synonymous with the ability to pause in the air? (5)

285. Great influence was brought to bear upon the French church to allow the illustrious ballerina Marie Camargo to be buried as a virgin. Why was that necessary? (3)

286. Some of the greatest ballet music ever composed is found in act 2 of Gluck's opera *Orfeo ed Euridice.* In this century, Balanchine has choreographed it for the Metropolitan Opera and Violette Verdy has danced the solo. Can you name the soloist in the premiere of the French version which Gluck presented in 1774? (The earlier version did not include the ballet.) (8)

287. Dance is a very popular art form today, but when was the only instance the British Parliament suspended a sitting so that members could attend the performance of two ballet stars? (7)

288. What was the scandal of the Hôtel de l'Académie Royale? (8)

289. What eighteenth-century ballerina was the subject of operas and a ballet? (3)

290. Here is a rather unusual admission from a dancer: To whom was eminent dancer Maximilien Gardel referring when he wrote in 1775 that, "he divined what the dancers themselves did not know . . . we look upon him rightly as our first master"? (5)

291. For a dancer, the interruption of her career is only one of the hazards of childbirth. Eighteenth-century singer and wit Sophie Arnould once commented on the many pregnancies of a particular ballerina: "She was like certain nations, always extending her borders, but never retaining her conquests." We'll give you 7 points if you can name the ballerina, and another 2 if you name her most famous offspring. (9)

292. Who was the dancer who boasted: "There are only three great men in Europe—myself, Voltaire, and the King of Prussia"? (3)

293. One of the old traditions still maintained at the Paris Opéra is the ranking system. As in the heyday of ballet in Paris, female dancers are not called ballerinas, but "étoiles" or stars. Can you give the other rankings for women in descending order, beginning with the top rank which we'll start you off with: "première danseuse étoile"? (20)

294. Here is a question from the popular ballerina and principal of the New York City Ballet, Violette Verdy, who wrote: "The Paris Opéra, founded in 1669 as the Académie Royale de Musique et de Danse existed for twelve years before the first professional ballerina was allowed to appear there.

    A. Who was the first ballerina? (9)

    B. Who was the first woman director of the Paris Opéra Ballet?" (3)

295. Who was the very famous man who made his first solo appearance as a dancer in the ballet *Cassandre?* (8)

296. Managers and impresarios of ballet companies have as much trouble today with dancers who skip rehearsals or performances as did their counterparts in the eighteenth century. However, eighteenth-century managers had a big advantage: they could threaten the intransigeants with "La Force" and "For-l'Évêque." What did this mean? (4)

297. Some dancers just won't take no for an answer. Gaetano Vestris implored Gluck to compose a chaconne for *Iphigénie* so that he could execute his leaps and other feats. The horrified composer, who was in the middle of reforming opera by eliminating gratuitous displays by singers and dancers, did not take kindly to the suggestion and exclaimed "A chaconne! Would the Greeks have had one?" What did the undaunted Vestris answer? (5)

298. Many choreographers have used Beethoven's symphonic music for ballets. Yet Beethoven actually composed two scores expressly as ballets that have received less attention from choreographers than his other music. Name them. (4)

299. There have been so many ballets based on Molière's *Le Bourgeois Gentilhomme* that it may surprise many to learn that the play was originally conceived and produced as a ballet to music by Lully. Who was the choreographer of the first *Le Bourgeois Gentilhomme* produced in 1670? (10)

300. What ballet position was inspired by the statue of Mercury by Giovanni da Bologna? (2)

301. A Danish sixteen-year-old made his ballet debut in *Armida* in 1821. He eventually became one of Denmark's most famous men. Who was the lad? (2)

302. Although Franz Joseph Haydn wrote no ballets, Balanchine among others has used his music. However, Haydn was more directly connected to the history of the dance since his personal valet and copyist was the father of a world-famous dancer. Can you name the dancer? (8)

303. Who was the first modern dancer? (5)

304. The 1653 *Ballet de la Nuit* was historic for two reasons. One was that Lully became court composer because of its success, directly influencing the course of ballet for two hundred years. The other reason was a nickname that resulted. Can you explain? (15)

Chapter Thirteen: Odd Facts and Strange Characters

Our last chapter includes all of the questions that we couldn't fit into any other categories. We think that these are some of the most interesting questions of all. Many of them concern the stars and companies of the previous chapters, but are included here so that the answers won't be too obvious.

305. Ballet audiences have always been amused by male dancers appearing in female roles, but can you name the dancer who had female breasts painted on him by none other than Picasso? (12)

306. What famous ballet company made up entirely of

THE PARISIAN POLKA.

children and celebrated for unusual precision was disbanded for moral reasons? (3)

307. What change at the Paris Opéra reputedly caused the Russians, English, and Austrians to threaten war with France? (7)

308. What dancer was called "fly-swallower" by his teacher? (3)

309. What dancer named her pet dog after a rival? (3)

310. Did you know that a dancer married the most famous economist of the twentieth century? For 5 points, name the economist and his ballerina bride. (5)

311. Identify the dancers as described below by their contemporaries:
  A. "Suddenly he soared upwards in a marvelous fashion that made him seem to have wings." (2)
  B. "His half-closed eyes gave an extraordinary, fascinating expression to his face." (1)
  C. "Academically such an exhibition of sheer acrobatics was inconsistent with purity of style: but the feat . . . had something elemental and heroic in its breathless daring." (2)

312. What ballerina was known as "The Richest Woman on the Stage"? (5)

The next series of questions is about ballet in the movies.

313. The most celebrated ballet film is the 1948 British movie, *The Red Shoes.* But did you know that previous ballets had been choreographed to the same story? What is the original source for the story of *The Red Shoes?* (3)

314. To date, the ballet dancer to have found the greatest success in the movies is Moira Shearer, the glamorous red-headed star of *The Red Shoes.* Can you name the one film she made in Hollywood? (3)

315. Who was the first famous dancer to dance in film? (Hint: She wasn't famous when she made the film.) (5)

316. Two questions about Charlie Chaplin's *Limelight:*
A. What famous ballet stars danced in *Limelight?* (4)
B. Who starred as the ballerina in the film? (1)

317. Who is the "I" in the film *I Am a Dancer?* (1)

318. Who plays a Russian ballet virtuoso called Petrov in the film *Shall We Dance?* (1)

319. Name the choreographer who staged the Babylonian scenes for D. W. Griffith's epic movie, *Intolerance.* (5)

320. Some questions about recent movies, *The Turning Point* and *Nijinsky:*
A. Who directed both films? (2)
B. Who portrayed the two feuding dancers in *The Turning Point?* (3)
C. Who portrayed Nijinsky and Karsavina in *Nijinsky?* (2)
D. Who portrayed Diaghilev in *Nijinsky?* (1)

321. What dancer starred in the film *Black Tights?* (3)

322. What ballerina portrayed Anna Pavlova in a 1953 film? (2)

323. Soviet film director Alexei Kvanihidze was married to what famous ballerina? (2)

324. What ballerina appeared in an Alfred Hitchcock thriller? (4)

325. No, not even ballet was spared the 3-D movie craze of the 1950s. What was the first 3-D ballet film? (9)

326. A. Who choreographed many of the fabulous dance routines for the Fred Astaire/Ginger Rogers RKO musicals of the 1930s? (5)

  B. What was the first movie to feature choreography by Busby Berkeley? (2)

327. What does the fictional spy James Bond have in common with ballet? Still confused? We'll make it easier. The choreographer of the James Bond movie *Live and Let Die* (1973) has also choreographed works for Alvin Ailey's company and for the Dance Theater of Harlem. Can you name the choreographer? (2)

328. This question was sent in by Walter Terry, the eminent ballet historian and critic, who has authored twenty-one books on the dance. Can you name the title of Walter Terry's first dance book? (3)

329. This one is easy if you know your mythology. What is the name of the muse of the dance? (1)

330. Leslie Caron and Shirley MacLaine are two famous actresses who began their careers in ballet, but can you name the dancer who left the Royal Danish Ballet to become world famous as an Ibsen actress (she created Nora in *The Doll's House*)? (5)

331. Nothing looks easier or more graceful in ballet than the support given by a good male partner when the ballerina is executing pirouettes, but this can be a dangerous task. Who was the partner who had his four front teeth knocked out by a ballerina who raised her elbow too high? (6)

332. What ballet company has had a play written about its creation? (2)

333. Dancing takes talent, but what premier danseur played the violin as well as danced in certain performances? (6)

334. What ballet star began his career as an Olympic athlete? (7)

335. What producer hasn't wanted a guaranteed success? The claque, or group of hired applauders, is a tradition that goes back to Nero's Rome. However, it was in 1820 that a man named Sauton organized a firm called "L'Assurance des succès dramatiques." Claiming to "assure your dramatic success," the organized claque rose to great power especially under the talented management of one particular man. In fact, he became so powerful that he ended up richer than most of the managers and stars he extorted money from. His story is immortalized in Balzac's *Lost Illusions*. While balletomanes dream about what nineteenth-century dancers they would like to see, we have no doubt that today's managers would most like to bring back the man who was known as "The King of the Claque." Can you name him? (8)

336. While not always known for their literary accomplishments, some dancers have written important books. Name the dancer-authors of:
  A. *Theatre Street.* (1)
  B. *Dance to the Piper.* (1)
  C. *Dancing in Petersburg.* (1)
  D. *Letters on Dancing.* (1)
  E. *To Dance.* (1)
  F. *History of Russian Ballet.* (1)

337. Many mothers have had to bear the bad news that their daughters would never make it as dancers; some have been wise enough not to listen. What later great ballerina's mother ignored the advice given by a ballet master to "make your daughter a dressmaker"? (3)

338. What great ballet composer contemptuously dismissed dancing as "no more than knowing how to bend and straighten the knees at the proper time"? (5)

339. Ironically, the grim purges that took place in the Soviet Union from 1937 to 1939, known as "Stalin's Great Terror," were caused in part by the assassination of a man whose name is immortalized in the annals of ballet history. Can you explain? (9)

340. In the early part of the twentieth century, an influential dance system was Eurhythmics. Who invented this system? (4)

341. Why did the beautiful Rosita Mauri, an étoile at the Paris Opéra of the 1880s and 1890s, vow never to eat any more caviar? (5)

342. Who was the first Russian ballerina to dance at the Paris Opéra? (6)

343. What was the philatelic distinction of Danish ballerina Margrethe Schanne? (3)

344. Fortunate are the dance students who are given correct advice. The following precepts for dancers are guaranteed to provide success—if the student can achieve them. Identify the author of each of the pearls of wisdom listed below:

> A. "A good dancer should serve as a model for the sculptor and painter." (2)

B. "Master technique and then forget all about it and be natural." (1)

C. "Keep an easy grace throughout the most exhausting steps." (3)

345. Before jogging, there were dance classes. What dancer began his ballet studies only to improve his ill health, but ended up by becoming one of the top male stars of his generation? (2)

346. Whose home in Russia was known as the "Athens of Perm"? (4)

347. Who founded the London Festival Ballet? (4)

348. What was the name of England's Royal Ballet before it was granted its royal charter? (1)

349. What is the oldest ballet company still active in England? (3)

The next two questions feature food for dance lovers.

350. What ballerina had her ballet shoes cooked and eaten by balletomanes? (3)

351. Have you ever seen Chicken Tetrazzini or Spaghetti Caruso on a menu and wondered why ballet stars are not honored in food the way opera singers are? Perhaps it's because dancers have to watch their weight (or maybe because balletomanes will eat a dancer's shoe). In any case, the great nineteenth-century French chef, Escoffier, listed four dishes in his *Guide to Modern Cookery* named after one legendary French dancer. Who was the dancer given such a tasty honor? (5)

352. Olympic champion skater John Curry owes much of

"PAS DE PATINEURS," IN THE NEW BALLET, AT HER MAJESTY'S THEATRE.

his style to ballet and has had ballet choreographers create some of his routines. But he was not the first skater to do so. Who choreographed ice-skating ballets for Sonja Henie? (3)

353. Perhaps the most famous dance contest in the world is the Varna International Ballet Competition. It is not surprising that this competition with Ulanova as the leading judge has awarded the most medals to Russians. The dancers of what country have won the second-most medals to date? (4)

354. Few dancers have not had some embarrassing moments on stage, but here's one that would be hard to top: "He made his appearance in a fine pas . . . but unluckily, in one of his most graceful pirouettes, a very important part of his drapery . . . became suddenly rent in a most unmendable manner. Shouts of laughter and applause followed which Monsieur (who had a very high opinion of himself) imagined were given for his jumping, nor was the supposition at all unjustifiable, for the higher he jumped, the more he was applauded. At last someone . . . called him off the stage . . . he was so shocked at the mishap . . . that he could never be induced to appear again." Take 25 points if you can identify the poor fellow. (25)

355. Edward Villella, the superb American dancer, has been something of an ambassador for ballet on talk shows and in interviews, and he has caught the American public's imagination by comparing dance to athletics. Villella has spoken of his fondness for football and basketball because of the grace involved in those sports. However, he was not the first to make the comparison. What other famous male dancer observed, "The thing that appealed to me about the game was the fact that it was the whole team which seemed to count, rather than any individual player no matter how brilliant. . . . With us, as with your football players, it is the entirety of effect which counts rather than the superlative excellence of any individual"? (8)

356. Legendary conductor Arturo Toscanini had what celebrated ballerina for a daughter-in-law? (3)

357. What famous male ballet role was until recently danced only by females? (3)

358. The chances are that if you mention ballet music, you will think of Tchaikovsky's great scores, yet another composer wrote a ballet score Tchaikovsky thought so highly of that he called *Swan Lake* "trash in comparison." Can you name the ballet and composer? (4)

359. Rankings have always been as important to dancers as to soldiers, but as one of the highest ranking dancers pointed out in her autobiography, "If generals were common in Russia, there were only five or six ballerinas, and one prima ballerina alone. . . ." Who were the only two officially designated Prima Ballerina Assoluta? (3)

360. Who was the first American ballerina to achieve the highest rank at the Paris Opéra, première danseuse étoile? (5)

361. Who was the only ballerina ever given the rank of prima ballerina of the Royal Danish Ballet? (3)

362. Lotte Goslar, student of Wigman and a popular dancer/mime, had two very famous pupils. Who were they? (8)

363. This pupil and assistant of Rudolf von Laban was the most important influence on modern dance in Germany. Her school, a mecca for modern dancers, was forced to close because of the disfavor of the Nazi regime. One of her last performances took place at the 1936 Berlin Olympics. Who was she? (2)

364. Can you name the dancer who made her ballet debut

at the age of six, became première danseuse of the Madrid Opera at the age of eleven, and then gave up classical ballet three years later to become perhaps the greatest Spanish dancer of all time? (2)

365. We've noted that dancers are beautiful people but one American dancer made sure that there weren't any doubts about it, touring for years billed as "the most beautiful man in the world." Can you name this Adonis? (3)

366. Who was the modest performer who advertised that he could "dance better than any living songwriter, and write a song better than any dancer on earth"? (2)

367. What Austrian dancer was known as the "Ambassadress of the Viennese waltz"? (2)

368. Who were the first Soviet dancers to tour the United States? (2 points each, for total of 4)

369. What dancer starred in Leonard Bernstein's *Mass?* (2)

370. The Netherlands Dance Theater created a sensation in a ballet by Glen Tetley called *Mutations.* Why? (3)

371. Who composed the score for the 1963 ballet *Mods and Rockers?* (2)

372. What native dance features a kind of on-point dancing for men that predates the on-point dancing of classical ballet? (3)

373. Who invented the leotard? (2)

374. Degas was inspired by ballet in the many masterful drawings, paintings, and sculptures he did of dancers. Name two ballets that were inspired by Degas's work. (5)

SCENE FROM THE NEW BALLET OF "LALLA ROOKH," AT HER MAJESTY'S THEATRE.

375. Fred Astaire received ballet training from a man who had been a favorite pupil of Enrico Cecchetti (in fact, Cecchetti's adopted son). Who was he? (10)

376. This is your last chance, so if you need some points, identify the following dancers whose given names as opposed to stage names are listed below. We'll give you 5 points for each correct answer, for a possible total of 80 points.

A. Abdulla Jaffa Anver Bey Khan.
B. Ottilia Ethel Leopoldine.
C. Mildred Herman.
D. Marcia Pereira de Silva.
E. Nora Koreff.
F. Roberta Sue Ficker.
G. Tula Ellice Finklea.
H. Edris Stannus.
I. Peggy Hookham.
J. Nelly Guillerm.
K. Sydney Francis Patrick Chippendall Healey-Kay.
L. Lillian Marks.
M. Eva Brigitte Hartwig.
N. Hilda Munnings.
O. Belton Evers.
P. Lynn Springbett.

Part III: Answers

Chapter Twelve: Historical Anecdotes and a Smattering of Technique

259. *Ballet Comique de la Reine* by Beaujoyeux.

260. L'Académie Royale de Danse founded by Louis XIV.

261. Mrs. Ekstrom's answer: "Fanny Bias and Geneviève Gosselin who first attempted it, and Amalia Brugnoli who astounded the public in Vienna, Italy, and London with her mastery."

262. "Gaetano Vestris and his son, Auguste.
Jean Petipa and two sons, Marius and Lucien.
Thomas Nijinsky and his son, Vaslav.
Jacques D'Amboise and his son, Christopher."
Take the points if you came up with those four or any other famous father-and-son dancers.

263. Carlotta Grisi, among the greatest of romantic ballerinas, might easily have become a famous singer as did her cousins, Giulia and Giuditta Grisi.

264. *Le Triomphe de l'Amour* in 1681.

265. When Guimard was twenty years old, she had her portrait painted and used it throughout her career as a guide for her stage makeup. No one was permitted to watch her in her dressing room. The notion was sound and could be used

today since a good portrait (using the same pigments as are used in makeup) tells more about color and contour than does a color photograph.

266. Carlotta Grisi.

267. Anna Heinel (1753-1808). The greatest German ballerina of her day, she was described by Horace Walpole as "the most graceful figure in the world, with charming eyes, bewitching mouth, and lovely countenance." She married Gaetano Vestris (but was not the mother of his famous son, Auguste).

268. The father was Gaetano Vestris and his son, Auguste.

269. Clotilde-Augustine Mafleurai's flowery name could not mask her very, very bad body odor. She tried everything to disguise her smell, even musk, but to no avail. Although partnerless, she was nevertheless a highly regarded premier sujet of the Paris Opéra from 1810 to 1818.

270. The rivalry between Marie Sallé (1707-1756) and Marie Camargo (1710-1770).

271. *The Bird Catcher.*

272. By enrolling her as a danseuse at the Paris Opéra. Since the Opéra was under the control of the king and not under civil authority, there was no way a profligate noble could be brought to justice.

273. Maximilien Gardel removed his mask in a 1772 performance of *Castor et Pollux* so that he would not be mistaken for Vestris. (If you said Vestris, though, take the points since even the authoritative *Concise Oxford Dictionary of Ballet* credits both dancers in separate entries with being the first to dance without a mask. Gaetano Vestris is supposed to have done it in *Médée et Jason,* but no date is given. Take your pick.)

274. The pas de bourrée—very fast little steps with the feet kept close together.

275. The pas de chat ideally resembles the movement a cat makes when jumping.

276. At the Paris Opéra, a beautiful dancer named Mlle Mariette caught her dress on the scenery while executing an entrechat and was rendered completely nude to the delight of at least half of the audience. The scandal led to an ordinance requiring "precautionary panties."

277. The *Ballet de Chevaux,* or *Ballet on Horseback,* was performed by knights riding on horses. The most famous *Ballet de Chevaux* was performed at the wedding of Leopold I and Margharita Theresa of Spain in 1666. The Lipizzaner horses of the Vienna Riding Academy continue the tradition of the *Ballet de Chevaux* in our time.

278. Jean-Baptiste Lully. He couldn't have been very good though, since his clumsiness was a direct cause of his death, from gangrene after stabbing himself with a baton while conducting.

279. Arthur Saint-Léon, who was a far better dancer than Lully, but not quite as good a composer.

280. This is the nickname given to the lowest-ranked dancer at the Paris Opéra. The writer Castil-Blaze noted it was due to their lean look and tendency always to be nibbling at something.

281. Louis Dupré (1697-1774) was the first, followed by

Gaetano Vestris (1728-1808) and his son, Auguste (1760-1842). It was a long time before the fourth, Nijinsky, came along in 1889.

282. Madeleine Guimard. The remark was by Sophie Arnould, one of the great opera singers of the day.

283. Entrechats.

284. Jean Balon (1676-1739). A great favorite of King Louis XIV, his name was possibly the inspiration for the term "ballon," meaning the ability to pause mid-air while jumping or leaping.

285. Marie Camargo (1710-1770), one of the first of the prima ballerinas, was said to have had a thousand and one lovers in her day. The last of them used his considerable influence to obtain the burial honors for the dancer, all the more unusual as the church rarely permitted dancers to be buried in hallowed ground.

286. Anna Heinel.

287. In 1781, Parliament called off its session so that the members could see the extraordinary performances of Gaetano Vestris and his son, Auguste, dancing together.

288. The Hôtel de l'Académie Royale was the rehearsal building for the Paris Opéra. At a party given there that included the celebrated composer Campra, the singer Mlle Pélissier, and the ballerina Camargo, the director suggested that the ladies remove their clothes and they gladly obliged. The orgy that resulted was so scandalous that Louis XV—thought to be furious at not being invited—fired director Gruer.

289. Marie Camargo. The ballet was choreographed by Petipa.

290. Jean-Philippe Rameau (1683-1764) was the successor to Lully as the first composer in France and one of the greatest ballet composers of all time.

291. Marie Allard (1742-1802) finally lost her figure and the affections of her most powerful lovers. Her son by Gaetano Vestris was the immortal Auguste, causing one of her conquests to regret that "he missed being my son by a mere fifteen minutes!"

292. The egotistical Gaetano Vestris was not really exaggerating; he was unquestionably the greatest dancer of his time, and only his son would later surpass him. Naturally, Gaetano had an equally glib explanation for the superiority of his son, Auguste: "He had an advantage over me since he had Gaetano Vestris for his father."

293. Première danseuse étoile
Première danseuse
Grand sujet
Petit sujet
Coryphée
Premier quadrille
Second quadrille
Élève (nicknamed "rat")
The terms, in masculine gender, also apply to the ranking of male dancers.

294. A. "Mlle de La Fontaine."
B. "Violette Verdy."

295. Louis XIV, the Sun King of France, loved ballets and fancied himself a pretty good dancer.

FANNY ELSSLER.

296. La Force and For-l'Évêque were greatly feared French prisons and many great dancers, including Mlle Théodore and Auguste Vestris, were carted there when they defied the authorities.

297. "They didn't have a chaconne?! Well, so much the worse for them."

298. *Ritterballett* (1791), and *The Creatures of Prometheus* (1801). Today, *Ritterballett* is seldom seen or even heard, but *The Creatures of Prometheus* is a concert favorite. It has received some ballet treatment lately, including one by Ashton for the Royal Ballet in 1970.

299. Pierre Beauchamp.

300. Attitude.

301. Hans Christian Andersen. He retained a lifelong interest in ballet as a friend of August Bournonville, but his fairy tales have had an even longer dance life as the inspiration for several ballets.

302. Fanny Elssler. Her father was Johan Elssler.

303. Henriette Hendel (1772-1849) specialized in "living pictures" inspired by ancient sculpture, Renaissance painting, and the posed attitudes of, among others, Lady Emma Hamilton (mistress of England's naval hero, Lord Horatio Nelson). Touring for over a decade in such expressionistic and in those days very disreputable performances, Hendel has been called the "eighteenth-century Isadora."

304. The star of the *Ballet de la Nuit* was Louis XIV. His performance in the final sequence as the Sun earned him his immortal nickname, "The Sun King."

THE VIENNESE CHILDREN, AT HER MAJESTY'S THEATRE.

Chapter Thirteen: Odd Facts and Strange Characters

305. Michel Pavlov in *Les Femmes de Bonne Humeur* first produced by Diaghilev in 1917. When Mme Cecchetti retired, the role was taken by Pavlov, who received expert help in making up from the current Diaghilev designer, Picasso.

306. The Danseuses Viennoises was made up of forty-eight very young ladies and toured the United States in 1848. A charming Currier and Ives print commemorates their tour. The company was disbanded because of public objections to young children exposed to the "immorality" of a theatrical life.

307. The edict to forbid access backstage to anyone not employed at the Opéra was a move intended to curb the lechery of the patrons. The edict was lifted after many diplomatic threats and protests. This amusing anecdote was reported in Marcel Bouteron's *Danse et Musique Romantiques,* published in 1927.

308. Vaslav Nijinsky.

309. Marie Taglioni. Her dog was named not after Fanny Elssler, her fierce rival, but "Grisi" after Carlotta Grisi, the first Giselle.

310. John Maynard Lord Keynes married Lydia Lopokova of Ballets Russes fame.

311. A. Auguste Vestris, described by Marie Vigée-Lebrun, the French painter, in *Souvenirs.*
   B. Nijinsky, in *Nijinsky* by Romola Nijinsky.
   C. Karsavina describing Pierina Legnani's thirty-two fouettés, in *Theatre Street.*

312. Mathilde Kschessinska, who exclaimed "I adore gems!" to a reporter before her debut in London, as she showed off the famous million-rubles-worth of jewels given to her by the czar and other Russian nobles. Unfortunately for Kschessinska, the ballerina had to leave her valuable collection behind when she fled the revolution.

313. A fairy tale of the same name by Hans Christian Andersen.

314. *The Story of Three Loves.*

315. Ruth St. Denis for Edison in 1893. The young dancer was participating in the very birth of the film industry, since these are the earliest movies as we know the term.

316. A. Melissa Hayden and André Eglevsky.
   B. Claire Bloom.

317. Rudolf Nureyev.

318. Fred Astaire. In his few opportunities to execute classical steps, Astaire does them very neatly with his special brand of magic, leaving little doubt that he might have been a premier danseur if he had been so inclined.

319. Ruth St. Denis.

320. A. Herbert Ross.
   B. Anne Bancroft and Shirley MacLaine.
   C. George de la Pena was Nijinsky; Carla Fracci was Karsavina.
   D. Alan Bates.

321. Zizi Jeanmaire.

322. Tamara Toumanova, in *Tonight We Sing.*

323. Natalia Makarova. He was her second husband.

324. Tamara Toumanova played a cruel Soviet dancer in *Torn Curtain.*

325. *Black Swan* (1952). Adapted from the third act of *Swan Lake,* it starred Beryl Grey. You can imagine the audience wearing those red and green cardboard glasses counting fouettés.

326. A. Hermes Pan.
   B. *Whoopee!* in 1930.

327. Geoffrey Holder.

328. *Invitation to Dance.*

329. Terpsichore.

330. Betty Schnell (1850-1939).

331. This was the unfortunate Nicholas Legat. The ballerina was Preobrajenska, who fainted when she saw his bloody mouth and realized what she had done.

332. The Royal Ballet, in a play called *Birth of the Royal Ballet,* produced in 1972.

333. Arthur Saint-Léon. The talented choreographer of *Coppélia* was one of the leading male dancers of his time. He played the violin expertly in the ballet *Le Violon du Diable,* which he danced with his wife, Fanny Cerrito.

334. Igor Youskevitch was a member of the 1932 Yugoslavian Olympic team participating in the Prague Games. Gold-medal skater John Curry, of course, has danced as a guest star with ballet companies, but cannot properly be termed a ballet dancer.

335. Auguste, who died in 1844. Auguste's power was absolute and no dancer could afford to ignore his demands; it was even said that he could cause a performance to be greeted with complete silence, an effective lesson for any would-be star.

336. A. Tamara Karsavina.
B. Agnes de Mille.
C. Mathilde Kschessinska.
D. Jean-Georges Noverre.
E. Valery Panov.
F. Serge Lifar.

337. This bad advice was given to the mother of Marie Taglioni.

338. Jean-Philippe Rameau.

339. After the murder of Communist party leader Kirov, the authorities changed the name of the venerable Maryinsky (then known as the State Academic Theater for Opera and Ballet). Kirov had no other connection with the ballet.

340. Émile Jaques-Dalcroze. It was a system of dance through musical rhythms and Diaghilev was so impressed with it that he hired the young Marie Rambert, a pupil of Jaques-Dalcroze, to teach it to Nijinsky.

341. Mauri became angry when she saw the czar carrying on a conversation in the royal box instead of watching her dance.

342. Tatiana Smirnova in 1844, whose lack of success did not discourage other Russians from ultimately triumphing there.

343. Margrethe Schanne was the first dancer to be immortalized on a Danish postage stamp!

344. A. Carlo Blasis in *Code of Terpsichore.*
      B. Anna Pavlova quoted by Victor Dandré in *Anna Pavlova.*
      C. August Bournonville in *Études Chorégraphiques.*

345. André Eglevsky.

346. The home of Serge Diaghilev.

347. Dame Alicia Markova.

348. The Sadler's Wells Ballet.

349. The Ballet Rambert, founded by Dame Marie Rambert in 1926.

350. Marie Taglioni. After she left Russia in 1842, the contents of her Russian home were auctioned off and her shoes were bought for two hundred rubles by balletomanes, who cooked and ate them with a special sauce.

351. Marie Camargo. Escoffier listed these Camargo dishes: Bombe Camargo, Filet de Boeuf Camargo, Ris de Veau Grillés Camargo, Soufflé à la Camargo. He also featured dishes named for romantic ballets: Bombe Coppélia, Omelette Sylphides, Sylphides de Volaille.

352. Catherine Littlefield.

353. Cuba.

354. The unlucky dancer was Monsieur La Croix. The amusing anecdote is related by the great Mozart tenor, Michael Kelly, in his entertaining *Reminiscences.*

355. Vaslav Nijinsky, quoted in the Diaghilev *Ballet Russe Courier,* of December, 1916.

356. Cia Fornaroli (1888-1954). A pupil of Cecchetti, she danced with Pavlova and was prima ballerina of the Metropolitan Opera and La Scala. She married Toscanini's son, Walter.

357. The role of Franz in *Coppélia,* choreographed in 1870 when male dancing had become almost nonexistent, was created in Paris by Eugénie Fiocre. In fact, the first time Franz was ever danced by a male at the Paris Opéra was eighty years later, in 1950, by Jean-Paul Andréani, danseur étoile of the Opéra.

358. *Sylvia* by Léo Delibes.

359. Pierina Legnani and Mathilde Kschessinska were both awarded the title of Assoluta by the Czar of Russia. Kschessinska, author of the quote regarding generals and prima ballerinas, further stated in *Dancing in Petersburg,* "The ballet world is like the rest of the Russian emigré world, in which the titles of count, prince, and colonel are appropriated without any right at all."

360. Marjorie Tallchief, who held the high rank at the Paris Opéra from 1957 to 1962.

361. Margot Lander (1910-1961) was awarded the title in 1942. There is little doubt that the title would have been awarded much earlier to Denmark's most famous dancer, Lucile Grahn (1819-1907), but Grahn quarreled with Bournonville early in her career and left Denmark in 1838 never to return.

362. Marilyn Monroe and Gower Champion.

363. Mary Wigman (1886–1973).

364. La Argentina (1890-1936).

365. Paul Swan (1883-1972).

366. George M. Cohan, the "Yankee Doodle Boy," who placed the ad because his fellow songwriters complained that he was a decent dancer, but a lousy songwriter, while his fellow hoofers thought he was a good songwriter, but a lousy dancer. Later, they all decided he was pretty good at both.

367. Grete Wiesenthal, who with her sisters developed a technique still taught in Vienna. Grete Wiesenthal choreographed the *Jedermann* productions for the Salzburg Festival in the 1930s.

368. Vakhtang Chaboukiani and Tatiana Vetcheslova in 1934.

369. Judith Jamison. Alvin Ailey was the choreographer.

370. It was danced in the nude.

371. The Beatles.

372. The traditional dances of the Ukrainian cossacks include dancing on their toes in soft leather boots.

373. Jules Leotard (1830-1870), a noted French acrobat.

374. *Entre Deux Rondes* by Serge Lifar.
Foyer de la Danse by Sir Frederick Ashton.

375. Luigi Albertieri had toured with his adopted father, had been a premier danseur in London, and had been the ballet master of the Chicago Lyric Opera and the Metropolitan Opera before opening his New York school.

376. A. Robert Joffrey.
B. Tilly Losch.
C. Melissa Hayden.
D. Marcia Haydée.
E. Nora Kaye.
F. Suzanne Farrell.
G. Cyd Charisse (who made her debut with Colonel de Basil's Ballet Russe after studying with Nijinska and Bolm).
H. Dame Ninette de Valois.
I. Dame Margot Fonteyn.
J. Violette Verdy.
K. Anton Dolin.
L. Dame Alicia Markova.
M. Vera Zorina.
N. Lydia Sokolova (Diaghilev named her after a famous Russian ballerina of the 1870s).
O. Erik Bruhn.
P. Lynn Seymour.

Add up your points and see how you rate.

Score:_____

Total:_____

SCENE FROM THE NEW BALLET OF " LA ESMERALDA," AT HER MAJESTY'S THEATRE.

Evaluation

0 to 500 points: Level 1—Mother made you take ballet lessons.

501 to 1,200 points: Level 2—You saw *The Turning Point.*

1,201 to 1,955 points: Level 3—A real balletomane.

1,956 points: Level 4—A perfect score is the mark
of a ballet-book author.

17/4